This project was made possible through the generosity of the following companies:

Your Pet, Our Passion.™

WEBSHOTS

Lexar™

Adobe

MIRRA™

Google™

BARk
the dog culture magazine

jetBlue
AIRWAYS®

DOG STAR
"I just wanted to throw Frisbees to dogs to meet girls," says David DeMent. "And then I found out I had this Michael Jordan dog." Flyin' Nash, a Texas heeler, caught his first Frisbee when he was just 7 months old.
Photo by Mark Almond, The Birmingham News

DOGS 24/7

Extraordinary Photographs of Wonderful Dogs

Created by Rick Smolan and David Elliot Cohen

CHRONICLE BOOKS
SAN FRANCISCO

Created by Rick Smolan and David Elliot Cohen

24/7 Media, LLC
PO Box 1189
Sausalito, California 94966-1189
www.america24-7.com

"Love Is Never Having to Say Anything at All"
by Patricia B. McConnell, PhD, from *Dog Is My
Co-Pilot: Great Writers on the World's Oldest
Friendship*, published by Crown, 2003. Copyright
© by Patricia B. McConnell, PhD. Reprinted by
permission of the author.

Library of Congress Cataloging-in-Publication
Data available.
ISBN 0-8118-4816-7

Manufactured in China

Distributed in Canada by
Raincoast Books
9050 Shaughnessy Street
Vancouver, British Columbia V6P 6E5

10 9 8 7 6 5 4 3 2 1

Chronicle Books, LLC
85 Second Street
San Francisco, California 94105
www.chroniclebooks.com

Pages 2–3
DOG AND PONY SHOW
April, a 2-year-old Lab mix, romps around with
Sam, a 6-year-old Welsh pony stallion, at Fox
Cry Farm in Virginia. Living with 20 horses
and no other dogs, April often races her big-
ger and ultimately faster friends.
Photo by Scott Elmquist

Table of Contents

CAPTIVATING CANINES
"I think we are drawn to dogs because they are the uninhibited creatures we might be if we weren't certain we knew better."
—George Bird Evans, Author.
Photo by Monty Lewis

ENERGIZER PUPPY
Joy is a yard full of bubbles for Maddie Hadwen
of North Berwick, Maine, and her Jack Russell
terrier Buster, who bites them as they float by.
Photo by Thatcher Hullerman Cook,
Thatcher Cook Photography

ALL ABOARD!
Clients of Best Friends, a dog day care center in Seattle, wait in the company's pickup while co-owners Marie Emery and Shellie Sarff round up the rest of their 20 charges after an hour at Blue Dog Pond. While humans are around, the animals remain civil: "They know we're the alpha dogs," says Sarff.
Photo by Alan Berner

CAJUN ROOTS
On his New Orleans vacation Seedy Njie wasn't looking for a pet, but when he came across a newborn pup in a vacant parking lot, his heart melted. He took her back to Georgia and named her Cajun to honor her Big Easy roots.
Photo by Sunny H. Sung,
The Atlanta Journal-Constitution

The Wonder of Dogs

By Mark Derr

Photo by Craig Fritz

I t's a cool, clear winter morning in Miami, and Kate is jazzed. Sprinting into an open field, the little black and tan Australian kelpie turns her head and deftly snags a tennis ball over her right shoulder. An elderly doctor and his wife pause to watch her pluck another ball from the air with a twisting leap.

A neighbor stops to talk and quickly is enlisted. A young boy rides up on his bicycle. Kate puts the ball at his feet and backs off, staring at it intently, tail wagging. The boy hesitates, then picks up the ball and unleashes a blooper. Snapping it up, Kate gives the ball back to our strong-armed neighbor. "She should be playing centerfield for the Marlins," the doctor says.

Kate is a virtuoso of the tennis ball. People delight in her agility, her speed, her skill in catching, dribbling, and then, with a forward thrust of her head, throwing the ball with remarkable accuracy up to 4 feet. Kate even lures people like our friend Susi, who "doesn't get the dog thing," into her game—and it is her game.

In such mundane exchanges, I believe, lies the key to our ancient, mutually beneficial relationship with dogs. Independent of training or coaching, dogs and humans have an almost mystical ability to form an instant rapport. With its keen nose; sharp ears; knack for hunting, retrieving, and hauling; and its utility in warning of intruders, the dog extends our senses and abilities. In the best case, we use our big brains to improve the dog's life. To a remarkable degree the dog understands verbal and nonverbal cues—our gestures, movements, and even our schedules—in a way no other animal can match. We, in turn, will follow a dog's gaze, read its body language, and decipher the meanings of its barks, howls, growls, and chortles.

At its best, the bond between dog and human deepens until the two form a unit that is wondrous to behold. Praising his mongrel foundling, Snap, in the March 1857 issue of *Putnam's Monthly* magazine, an anonymous author spoke for men and women through the ages and across many cultures: "He is not a handsome dog, and he is not intelligent, and he is, so far as I know, entirely useless—not good for a thing—but he loves me and I love him, and he growls for me, and I growl for him, and wherever I go he goes, and I am never desolate or forsaken."

Dog trainer Lourdes Edlin learned the depth of her bond with her big Labrador retriever, Cruiser, a few years ago, on the last day of a multi-event adventure competition (with dogs) held in Colorado. On a long climb that had turned brutally steep, Edlin "bonked," hit the wall. She hitched herself to Cruiser, so he could help her along, and almost immediately lost her footing on a ledge with a sheer 15-foot drop onto rocks. The 80-pound Cruiser braced himself and stood fast, muscles bulging, while Edlin used the leash to pull herself to safety. "He pulled me up the mountain after that and wouldn't leave my side," Edlin told me. "On the way down, he positioned himself between me and that same ledge to keep me from slipping."

Whether kelpie or Lab, lilliputian Chihuahua or rangy cur, the dog is essentially a gray wolf who tacitly agreed millennia ago to hitch its evolutionary fate to ours. When, where, why, or how wolf became dog is hotly debated. Dates for the dog's emergence range from 135,000 years ago to around 15,000 years ago in East Asia. I find the earlier date, based on genetic studies by evolutionary biologist Robert K. Wayne at the University of California at Los Angeles, most intriguing, not least because it suggests that dogs and modern humans evolved together.

It appears the tamest wolves, the ones least fearful of and most social toward humans and, thus, most likely to stay near a village, formed the core population of dogs, which quickly spread via trade and migration to other bands of people. By the end of the last ice age some 10,000 years ago, dogs had colonized the world with their human companions. Since then, through what Charles Darwin called conscious and unconscious selection, they have become as varied in size, shape, behavior, physical capability, and status as the cultures in which they dwell. They have served as companions, hunters, herders, guards, beasts of burden, foot warmers, guides for the quick and the dead, warriors in battle, gladiators, bull and bear baiters, and messengers. They have fished, turned spits and powered machines, provided hair for textiles, and saved lives.

Dogs came across the Bering Land Bridge with the first Americans, and they kept coming with each successive wave of immigrants. Each new group of dogs mixed with the local population, creating in the process a generalized mutt or cur—usually ginger, yellow, or spotted, medium to large in size—that was adept at most canine tasks. This was the nation's single most common dog until just after World War II.

In the years following the war, Americans created a car-based, metropolitan society. They curbed the free-roaming, free-breeding ways of country dogs and demanded purebred dogs to match their new lifestyle, believing they represented quality. Most of those breeds had been created or altered by wealthy sportsmen during the 19th century through extensive inbreeding and the use of "favored sires." These practices created dogs of great beauty and, sometimes, great ability—but also prone to debilitating genetic diseases like hip dysplasia. Overbreeding dogs for the show ring and pet market compounded the problem. To date, researchers have identified more than 350 canine genetic ailments, many specific to particular breeds.

By 2004, approximately half of America's 65 million dogs—most of them companions—were purebred, and demand continues to rise. But, increasingly, people are looking for working dogs, including curs, fueled by the belief that they are more physically and temperamentally sound. And growing numbers of people are seeking new activities for their dogs: herding and field trials; Frisbee and tennis ball chasing;

agility and other athletic competitions; visiting hospitals and nursing homes; assisting people with disabilities; tracking endangered species in order to protect, not kill, them; hazing nuisance birds and deer; searching for victims of disasters; and serving as scent detectors. At the same time, hunting, racing, pulling sleds, and other sports and activities traditionally associated with dogs have come under fire from animal-rights activists who argue that they are inherently cruel.

The Delaware Indians believed that dead dogs guarded the path across the Milky Way to the creator—and that they refused passage to the souls of people who had mistreated dogs. Wondrous though it can be, the dog-human relationship remains a work in progress. Today, too many dogs are fenced or crated and ignored. Reflecting their people, 24 percent are obese. Another 20 to 25 percent are psychologically "abnormal," suffering problems with aggression, anxiety, and phobias, like our late Chesapeake Bay retriever, Seneca, who was so terrified of thunder and other noises that she once tried to dive out of a second-story window and, another time, chewed through a chain-link fence.

Dogs are abandoned, abused, neglected, and killed, and, in turn, they spread disease, attack, harass, and, occasionally, even kill people, leading to legislation to ban certain breeds, like the pit bull. Each year, 2 to 3 million dogs are euthanized in shelters. Due to the rise in no-kill shelters and breed rescue clubs, that number is just a fraction of the 17 million killed annually through the 1980s, but still unacceptable to many dog lovers. Fully 25 to 30 percent of America's 65 million dogs, often surrendered for behavioral problems like excessive barking and aggression, have passed through shelters or breed rescue groups, served time as strays, or been adopted directly from individuals. Villain, for example, was a shelter dog, a female black Lab that a Florida firefighter trained to enter fire scenes where arson was suspected and sniff out the faintest remnants of flammable liquids. Like Villain, the majority of detector dogs—able to scent everything from contraband food to drugs to bombs with close to 98 percent accuracy—are adopted dogs, showing that what's undesirable in a family pet can be highly valued in other contexts.

At the same time, veterinary medicine is beginning to devise treatments for dog behavioral problems that may help reduce the number of rejected animals, as well as improve their overall physical health. Scientists have also begun to peel back some of the myths and legends about the evolution of dogs while continuing to probe the characteristics of dogs adept at certain tasks. Successful decoding of the dog genome should accelerate the search for the causes of genetic disease.

But science is unlikely to solve the most upsetting problem with dogs: their short life spans. Compared to humans, they don't live long enough, and their passing never gets easier to bear, especially when we have to decide that they are too old and frail, in too much pain to continue. The last time my wife, Gina, and I had to make that choice was with our fearless, aloof Catahoula Leopard dog, Marlow, who had presided over our lives for 14 years. He and his boon companion, Clio, another Leopard dog who had died old and decrepit six months earlier, had twice run off intruders, and, in a savage fight, had once prevented Gina from being mauled by a bull terrier. The day after we learned that I had Parkinson's disease he collapsed, and we carried him to the vet for a final good-bye.

Painful as those partings are, I can't imagine life without dogs. They are our link to the natural world, to a consciousness beyond our own. There are people who, for cultural and personal reasons, find dogs repulsive, or who, for philosophical reasons, would forbid the keeping of animals altogether. But I believe that we, as a species, would be diminished without them, trapped solely in a world of our own devise.

Katie barks, telling me it is time to play ball, and I will oblige, knowing that in a few years her voice will be stilled, and I will again be heartbroken but richer for having known her.

Mark Derr is the author of several books, including Dog's Best Friend *and, most recently,* A Dog's History of America. *A regular contributor to* The New York Times, *he is editor-at-large for* The Bark *magazine.*

Best Friends

UNCONDITIONAL LOVE
Kelsey Thornton, 8, cozies up to 4-year-old Nick, the family mutt. It is a symbiotic relationship: She gets a soft, warm cuddle, and he gets a good head scratch.
Photo by Stephen B. Thornton, Arkansas Democrat-Gazette

BOBBLEHEAD
During rides in the family sedan, Papa, a 5-pound Chihuahua, makes like a bobblehead on the rear deck while James Huerta, 11, indulges the attention hound.
Photo by Peter Casolino

PRETTY IN PINK
Ruth Carroll dawdles around her winter home
at the Lake Myers RV Park with her bichon frise,
named for novelist Danielle Steele.
Photo by Ted Richardson,
Winston-Salem Journal

TAKE ME TO THE RIVER

Five-year-old T'Pau, named after a Vulcan character on *Star Trek*, is fascinated by ships—though not the intergalactic variety. The Boston terrier is happiest sitting on a Riverside Park bench in Manhattan with Maki Fowler watching boats float by on the Hudson.
Photo by Barbara Alper

DANCING WITH WOLVES

Loki Clan Wolf Refuge co-owner Aimee Crosby and Atlas share a special bond. "His owner was killed in a barroom brawl, and I was the first person who paid attention to him," says Crosby. The New Hampshire nonprofit adopts unwanted wolf/dog crosses and educates the public about this trendy but difficult-to-manage mix.
Photo by Lloyd E. Jones, The Conway Daily Sun

TRUSTY COMPANION
Obediah Bauer, 13, and Jade take a breather after a game of tag. The boy's affection for the Airedale is no small accomplishment: Before his parents acquired Jade four years ago, Obediah had been bitten by three different dogs. Jade's mellow, steadfast manner eventually won the boy over.
Photo by Jerry Anderson

WHAT A KNOCKOUT!
"He looked like Mike Tyson punched him in the face, so I named him Tyson," says Noah Steere of his 6-month-old English bulldog. The professional bodybuilder always wanted a bulldog, but had to wait until he saved up $1,500 from his nutritional supplement business in North Carolina to afford the now-58-pound pooch.
Photo by Cindy Burnham, Nautilus Productions

NEW YORK GIANT
Whenever the weather's nice, Steve Wright, Linda Jerbic, and Gigi the Chihuahua take advantage of Manhattan's Union Square dog run. The fenced run in the heart of Manhattan allows city dogs the rare freedom to run and sniff to their hearts' content.
Photo by Andrew DeMattos

HEAD TO HEAD
Prized in Egypt and Africa for thousands of years, the basenji prefers hot, dry climates. Northern Maryland doesn't fit the bill, so Terry Sarber keeps Kylie swaddled inside his sweater during the Frederick County Humane Society Walk-N-Wag event.
Photo by Perry Thorsvik

PAMPERED PUG
Pit bulls may grow in Spanish Harlem, poodles may prance in outer borough parks, but Manhattan pugs convene at the dog run at Tompkins Square Park. This pampered pug hangs out in a form-fitting Baby Björn carrier.
Photo by Michael Harp

MIRACLE WORKER

During her daily visit to a Portsmouth, New Hampshire, day care center, Nellie communes with resident Zoe Pinione. As the story goes, soon after Nellie started her career as a therapy dog, she licked the face of a clinically depressed, bedridden man. "It's an angel!" the man shouted as he jumped out of bed.

Photo by Nancy G. Horton

BEACH BOY

Elizabeth Winston found Peanut, an abused stray, seven years ago in Puerto Rico. Steady affection from Winston and her partner, Zoe Lewis, helped the ex–street dog blossom into a cuddle-puss who revels in family outings to Herring Cove Beach in Cape Cod.

Photo by Vincent DeWitt,
Cape Cod Times

ACE PEST CONTROL

When Grayce Backstrom brought Challis home to the family's goat farm three years ago, she didn't know that the Parson Jack Russell would become one of the family's hardest-working farmhands—hunting mice, voles, and ground squirrels, and corralling goats.

Photo by William H. Mullins

A DOG'S LIFE

Frosty, an abandoned Australian shepherd mix, relishes the embrace of Gayle Morris, a supervisor at Wayside Waifs, a shelter in Kansas City, Missouri.

Photo by Tammy Ljungblad

LOST AND FOUND

Belle, a corgi/shepherd mix, was spayed by the Humane Society and never had any pups of her own. Enter Molly, an abandoned terrier/Chihuahua who recently joined the household. Molly rarely strays from her surrogate mom's proximity, preferring to snooze in the curve of her belly or perch on her warm back.

Photo by Sandy Huffaker

MUZZLE NUZZLE
Sadie, a barn dog at Beaver Creek Ranch in Kansas, licks Paige, a young paint horse. Surrounded by 11 horses and only one other dog, Sadie has adopted some of the behaviors of her equestrian companions. She eats carrots and goes for trail runs alongside the horses, doling out kisses on the way.
Photo by Teresa Gawrych

PICK ME! PICK ME!
Outside the K-9 Obedience Training Center in
Topeka, Kansas, American bulldog pups sell
themselves to passersby.
Photo by Chris Landsberger,
The Topeka Capital Journal

IDENTITY CRISIS

Someone forgot to tell Sassy she's not a cow. As the only canine at Ocean Breeze Farm in Westerly, Rhode Island, the 3-year-old border collie has bonded with the farm's 70 Holsteins and prefers their feed to her kibble.

Photo by William K. Daby

MEANWHILE, BACK AT THE RODEO...
Although dogs are supposed to work the cattle at rodeos, these new friends at the Western Regional Intercollegiate Rodeo in Elko, Nevada, would rather just sniff each other.
Photo by Jim Laurie, Stephens Press

MINNIE AND ME

After school, New Jersey seventh-grader Brady Dupre usually heads to Nicole Whitley's house to listen to music, watch TV, and hang out with Minnie, a miniature dalmatian. Dupre, who has never had a dog of her own, was born with a rare genetic disorder characterized by malformed limbs.

Photo by Peter Ackerman, Asbury Park Press

A BOY AND HIS DOG

David Hodge and dachshund Lucky attend the second annual Westmuttster Dog Show in Idaho Springs, Colorado. The fundraiser, benefiting the Clear Creek Animal Rescue League, features mutts and purebreds competing in categories like Worst Breath, Best Tail, and Best Costume (for which Lucky dressed as a caterpillar).

Photo by Trevor Brown, Jr.,
Rich Clarkson & Associates

SNAKE CHARMER
Four-year-old Michael Lee's pet python Sunshine and his rottweiler/bulldog pup Sid compete for attention. Truth be told, Sid and Sunshine find each other pretty uninteresting.
Photo by Bruce Strong, LightChasers

HOUND POUND

Kentucky breeder Dennie Skaggs guesses that 1 in 10 foxhounds has what it takes to become a fox chase champion. Given these odds, three or four of the dogs in his pack of 40 might bring home trophies from field trials held throughout Appalachia. A champion hound's offspring can fetch up to $10,000.

Photo by John Isaac

GREY EXPECTATIONS

"Greyhounds are like Lay's potato chips," says June Bazar. "You can't have just one." More than a greyhound mom, Bazar has been director of a greyhound adoption program at Lincoln Park, a top-rated Rhode Island dog track, for 24 years. China, Laddie, and Lilly are three of Bazar's four "babies."

Photo by John Freidah

CAMPFIRE GIRLS

Sasha Azel offers Flax a sniff of a delicately roasted marshmallow while her sister Yazi blackens another one.

Photo by José Azel, Aurora

MIDDLE EARTH

Dr. Larry Reynolds, a dedicated backcountry adventurer, hikes or skis every chance he gets. After ascending 1,000 feet on the rocky ridge trail in Alaska with his dog Frodo, he stops to make coffee in a white spruce forest.

Photo by Jim Lavrakas, Anchorage Daily News

DESERT SUNSET

Attended by his collie mix Beorn, college student Chris Meenach watches the sun fall behind New Mexico's San Andres Mountains.

Photo by Craig Fritz

THE LONELY SHEPHERD
Raised with sheep since birth, Julie instinctively guards her flock from predators on wide-open Wyoming rangelands. The dependable Akbash lives with the sheep and only sees rancher Mike Curuchet when he restocks her feed station. Before he bought his three Akbashes, Curuchet lost 300 lambs a year to coyotes. Now, he loses only a handful.
Photo by Bobby Model

WELCOME BACK
Over the past 30 years, Tom Harward earned such a reputation for adopting strays that townsfolk simply left unwanted dogs at the top of his driveway in Belington, West Virginia. Eventually, his wife said no more. Now a motley crew of eight meets Harward when he arrrives home from work each day.
Photo by Melissa Farlow, Aurora

The Wind in My Face

WHITE SNAPPER
From the safety of a Jeep Cherokee, feisty Lhasa apso Lilly hunts for passing cars. "She makes a little biting sound as each one goes by," says driver Katherine Holmes.
Photo by Katherine Holmes,
Mississippi State University

EASY RIDER
Elsa hitches a ride to the Pickens Flea Market with her buddy Red Gardner. On weekends, the speed-loving mutt moonlights as a registered South Carolina Therapy Dog at Greenville-area hospitals, where she visits with mentally ill and emotionally disturbed patients.
Photo by Owen Riley, Jr.

BOWWOW WOW!
Surf shorts, spa robes, pajamas, jeans—they're
all part of Tiki Beauzay's clothing line for dogs,
Gidget-Gear By Tiki. Her inspiration was her
Bedlington terrier Gidget. Beauzay sells her
original designs out of a small storefront in a
converted motel near Sarasota, Florida.
Photo by Chip Litherland,
Sarasota Herald-Tribune

DOGGLES

Buddy the boxer always hangs her head out the car window, only now she wears goggles. The vet recommended eyewear to keep bugs and dust from getting in her eyes. After a bit of trial and error, the Reichanandter family of Indiana found that goggles worn by jockeys suit Buddy best.

Photo by Jeri Reichanadter

RIDING BITCH

"I hold on and she holds on, too," says Patrick Perry of his favorite riding companion, Sheba. The American boxer was already well trained before Perry got the bike. "She took right to it," the Louisiana native says. The duo now performs in stunt competitions throughout the southern United States.

Photo by Arthur D. Lauck

Dog House

DOOR BELLES
West Highland white terriers Gertrude and Alice wait for Bill Kaiser to come home. The Westies are named for Lost Generation author Gertrude Stein—born a few blocks away in Pittsburgh's Mexican War Streets—and her partner Alice B. Toklas.
Photo by Annie O'Neill

LESS DANDER, MORE FUN
The Greene family hadn't had a dog because LeeAnn, hugging daughter Abby, is allergic. Enter the family's bichon frise, one of a handful of breeds advertised as hypoallergenic (others include poodles, Chihuahuas, and Wheaten terriers). Cubby's skin produces less sneeze-inducing dander than other dogs.
Photo by Bill Greene, The Boston Globe

WHO LET THE DOGS OUT?
Roscoe and Nipper bask on the couch after one of their excellent adventures. They dash out whenever the door is opened and return a few hours later, wet and muddy, and looking very proud.
Photo by Rikki Ward

OTTOMAN EMPIRE

Daisy, an Old English sheepdog who suffers from arthritis, taught herself to sit on a stool for relief. Despite her infirmity, Daisy is "good-natured and active," says her guardian James Smith of Dallas, Texas, "and she still tries to herd the kids."
Photo by James D. Smith

BEDTIME STORY

When Barbie Kirby was getting ready for bed, she found that Molly and her stuffed bear grabbed the prime pillow spot. Kirby suspects that the 2-year-old beagle mix just pretended to be asleep so she didn't have to move.

Photo by Barbara Kirby

FORTY WINKS

Wyoming animal shelter manager Corie Rybak brings her work home: Four of her six pets came from the shelter. A one-cat woman before she took the job five years ago, Rybak says her expanded family suits her just fine.

Photo by W. Garth Dowling

LET SLEEPING DOGS LIE

A year after relocating to Kentucky from Chicago, Sunnie has adjusted to the laid-back Southern lifestyle. In a bedroom the size of her old city yard, Sunnie keeps David Adams-Smith company on a lazy Sunday morning.

Photo by Jeanie Adams-Smith, Western Kentucky University

...AND I'M WORTH IT

These days, urban pets suffer more shampoo-
ing and primping than ever before—it's
enough to give a hound an identity crisis. So
how often should dogs get a scrub, anyway?
Whenever they're dirty, say experts. Chloe
Hill, 4, applies that rule of thumb to Saaboo
with a cool bath on the front lawn.

Photo by Philip Barr, The Birmingham News

CONEHEAD

Hapless Elsa came out on the losing end of a
skirmish with a backyard prickly pear cactus.
But her battle wounds weren't nearly as bad
as the undignified collar the vet attached to
stop Elsa from scratching her healing nose.
Nine-month-old Eli Sonnenmair, at least,
thought the new accessory was cool.
Photo by Jan Sonnenmair, Aurora

HURRY UP ALREADY!

Before heading out to the school bus stop to visit with all the kids, Lilly waits for Elizabeth Newton, 8, to load up her lunch box. The Newton family rescued Lilly from the pound in 2000.
Photo by Jonathan Newton

UNDERFOOT

Photographer Trevor Brown caught his rat terrier Jackson in a moment of repose during breakfast in his parents' kitchen in Denver. The energetic dog usually spends his days darting around the house and chasing squirrels in the backyard. "He's a total spaz," Brown says.
Photo by Trevor Brown, Jr.,
Rich Clarkson & Associates

POODLE RX

"I think we underestimate how much dogs mean to older people," says Helen O'Rourke-McClary, who takes Ashley, her 12-year-old red poodle, to visit the terminally ill in Florida hospices. When O'Rourke-McClary's husband passed away in 2002, Ashley was with him in the bed, and she continued to sleep there for the next three months.

Photo by Lexey Swall, Naples Daily News

SHE CAN'T SPELL...YET

Do not say s-h-o-e-s in front of Sadie, unless you're willing to take the Pekingese for a w-a-l-k. The linguistically advanced 6-year-old has a vocabulary of approximately 30 words, says guardian Carole Auld of Dover, Delaware.

Photo by Dee Marvin

GOLDEN GIRLS
Six-year-old Natasha Hunt Lee likes to dress up Lambchop when company comes over. The retriever is deaf, so Natasha lets her break a bunch of house rules, like "no dogs on the bed."
Photo by Michael Lambert

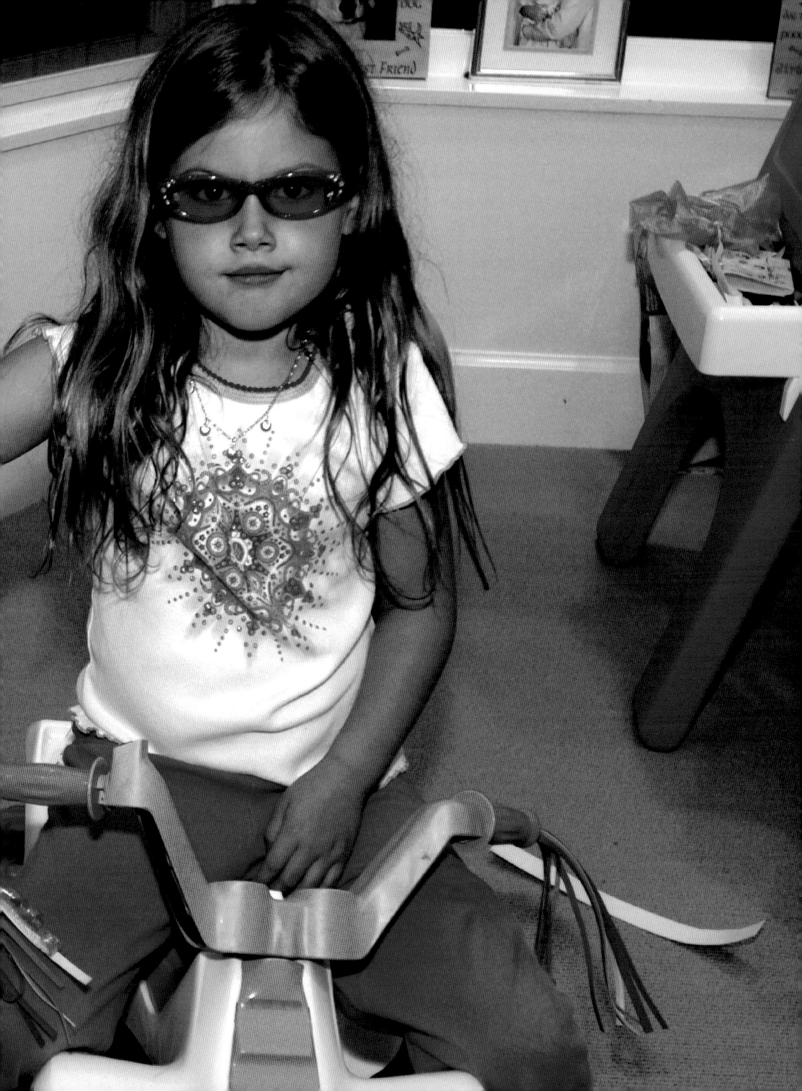

LAZY BOY
Eight-year-old Pink catches some z's in one of his three designated armchairs. When he's not snoozing—according to experts, the average house dog sleeps 14 hours a day—the mellow, 225-pound Harlequin Great Dane likes to watch the tube. His favorite network? *Animal Planet*. Seriously.
Photo by Douglas Kent Hall

ROOM WITH A VIEW

From Stephen Huneck's Vermont studio, Molly looks out at the rolling slopes of Dog Mountain. No kidding. Huneck, a canine-inspired folk artist best known for his children's books, named his 150-acre mountaintop farm in honor of his favorite subject.

Photo by Karen Pike,
Karen Pike Photography, Hinesburg

THE GRASS IS GREENER

When a plank fell from the Reichanadters' fence, they were going to fix it until they saw how much Starr liked peeking through. The Reichanadters adopted Starr from a family who kept her chained to her doghouse; it took two years for Starr to learn to play.

Photo by Jeri Reichanadter

SCREEN PASS
Southern swamp hunters favor the tenacious Catahoula Leopard dog, which, according to local lore, is a cross between domestic dogs raised by Indians of Louisiana's Catahoula Lake region and the Spanish war dog that arrived in the 16th century. The breed is the state dog of Louisiana.
Photo by David Grunfeld, The Times-Picayune

CREATURE COMFORTS

Ken, who camps out under the footbridges near Harvard Square, says his loyal cat and dog comfort him during tough times. But companion animals can also prevent itinerants like Ken from getting off the streets: A recent survey of homeless adults found that 95 percent would refuse any shelter that didn't welcome their pets.

Photo by Brian Clark

DOGVILLE

In 1997, the three human residents of a bend-in-the-road called Rabbit Hash, Kentucky, elected a mutt named Goofy to serve as the town's mayor, which he did, honorably, until his passing in 2001. During Goofy's regime, Rabbit Hash's handful of dogs—including Gussie, below—had it real good.

Photo by Patrick Reddy, Cincinnati Enquirer

LAP DOGS
Taco, a Chihuahua mix, and Spot, a Catahoula Leopard dog, may not know it, but they're boarding in the lap of luxury. As overnight guests at one of two Cozy Inn Pet Resort & Spas in Pennsylvania, they pad around on heated ceramic tile floors and watch their own TVs.
Photos by Jason Cohn, www.jasoncohn.com

MASSAGE ANYONE?

In the executive suite of the Stahlstown Cozy Inn, Princess dozes through a soap opera. Among the inn's indulgences are hot-oil coat treatments, Swedish massage, and a bone-shaped swimming pool. Princess's family, vacationing in the Caribbean for a week, paid $245 for the dog's vacation.

BACKCOUNTRY BARRACKS

"It's impossible to sneak up on this place," notes Frank Teasley, owner of Jackson Hole Iditarod Sled Dog tours and custodian of this kennel for 180 boisterous Alaskan huskies. During the busy winter season, Teasley's sled dogs cover 4,000 miles, pulling tourists through the frozen valleys of the Bridger-Teton National Forest.
Photo by W. Garth Dowling

HOUND MAINTENANCE
"Three were planned, the rest were accidents," says Ellen Hongo, who untangles her hounds during a deworming vet visit. Six of Hongo's nine purebreds were foster animals from Basset Rescue of Northern California. "People change the carpet, and the pet's hair doesn't match it anymore," Hongo explains. "So they dump the dog."
Photo by Jessica Brandi Lifland

FEAR ITSELF

Bojangles waits for his annual booster shots at a New Hampshire pet hospital. "He starts shaking as soon as he gets in the door," says companion Susan Sinclair.
Photo by Ben Garvin,
www.bengarvin.com

AN OUNCE OF PREVENTION

While his mom fills out medical forms, a puppy cowers against the wall of Boston's Angell Memorial Animal Hospital in anticipation of his immunizations. Early shots for distemper, hepatitis, and parainfluenza cost about $18 each, and expenses quickly add up: The average American dog owner spends $263 each year at the vet's office.
Photo by Sarah Brezinsky

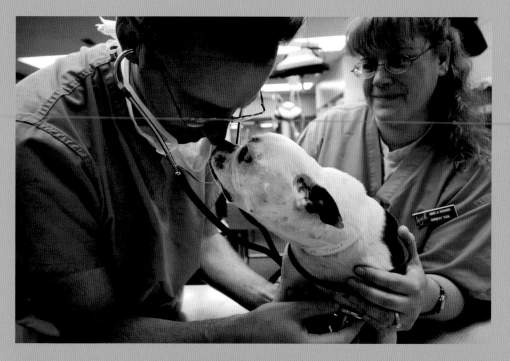

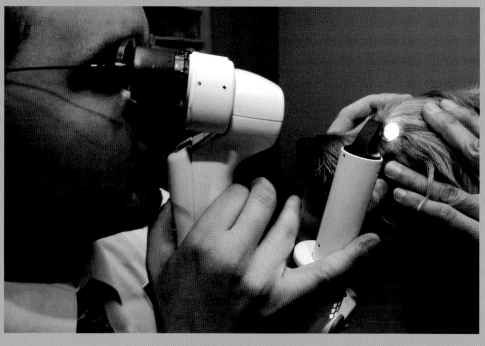

THE DOCTOR IS IN

Held by surgery technician Angela Richard, 9-month-old Angel sniffs out Dr. Nicholas Trout at Angell Memorial Animal Hospital. The Boston terrier pup has dislocated kneecaps, a common congenital condition in small dogs, and will be undergoing a $2,500 bilateral knee surgery.

Photos by Sarah Brezinsky

EYE SPY

After cataract surgery and plastic lens implants, Della, a 6-year-old Australian terrier, visits the animal hospital twice a year for eye examinations. Cataract removal is the most common surgery in the ophthalmology unit—and the most rewarding, says Dr. Daniel Biros. "Afterward, they can chase squirrels again."

HOUND'S TOOTH

With the help of Maria Wennerg and Jennifer Lomastro, Dr. Margo Roman performs dental work on a patient after administering a frankincense aromatherapy sedative. The vet offers acupuncture, massage, and Reiki (natural energy healing) in addition to traditional medical services. Business at her holistic clinic, Main Street Animal Services in suburban Boston, grew by 30 percent last year.

JACK OF ALL TRADES When not riding through the desert in his owner's ATV, Apachee, a Jack Russel terrier, participates in agility contests, works as a therapy dog, and water skis. *Photo by Susan Talarico*

TAKE A LOAD OFF, NELLIE During a strenuous hike up Kinder Scout mountain in Derbyshire, England, Wee Nellie, a Yorkshire terrier, prefers to go piggyback in owner Laura Armstrong's rucksack. *Photo by Laura Armstrong*

WO DOGS IN A TUB After a hot August afternoon spent herding cows, border collies Snoopy nd Heine cool off in a watering trough at the Crowley Ranch in Ontario, Oregon.
hoto by Katariina Sutphin

SURF'S UP "If he were human, he'd be a surfer," says Sharron Paris of her dog Max, who jumps n his float and coasts until he reaches shore. *Photo by Sharron Paris*

WINTER WONDERLAND Joseph sports snow wear on his first winter outing. The Coton de Tuleaur, known for their durability and quick-drying hair, originally came from Madagascar.
Photo by Kaoru Makiguchi

BEACH BABY On Tribble's first trip to the beach, the 4-month-old Pembroke Welsh corgi was so smitten with the sand that she didn't even venture into the water.
Photo by Anne Morton August

WINTER SOLACE In the spring, Darby searches for rabbits in the flatlands of Noblesville, Indiana. In the winter, he surrounds himself with the cool serenity of the snow.
Photo by Shirley A. Jones

LIFE IMITATES ART Mali, a plucky West Highland white terrier, sits fearlessly beside the FDR memorial's larger-than-life statue of Fala, the 32nd president's beloved scottie.
Photo by Wisit Singhsomroje

Working Like a Dog

AT THE ROUNDUP
Tide, a blue merle border collie whose owners traveled all the way to England to get him, is so enthusiastic about his job at the Deschambeault farm that he has to be brought inside at night so the sheep can get some sleep.
Photo by Lloyd E. Jones,
The Conway Daily Sun

WINTER WORK
Nunataks—sharp peaks shaped by retreating glaciers—dwarf a dog-mushing team skimming across Alaska's Juneau Icefield. Between May and September, dog teams employed by Era Helicopter Tours work 10-hour shifts, taking care of 300 tourists a day.
Photo by Michael Penn

FEELING SPECIAL

At a 4-H dog show in Ohio, Daisy, a spitz mix, took home a blue ribbon after executing long sit, long down, circle right, and circle left commands. Ashley John's training secret? "Make Daisy feel special but be strict."

Photo by Bruce Strong, LightChasers

BEST IN SHOW

Although beagles are known for their skills in the field, 5-year-old McHub excels at posing. Under the tutelage of Oklahoman Willis McWilliams, McHub has won Best Puppy, Best Male, and Best in Show at numerous National Kennel Club competitions.

Photo by Dan Hoke

WITH THE GREATEST OF EASE

A member of the RUFF Flyball Club of Englewood, Colorado, Maxx flies over a hurdle in the relay competition. The Jack Russell clears four hurdles, triggers a tennis ball release, and carries it back over the hurdles for his handoff.

Photo by Jamie Schwaberow, Rich Clarkson & Associates

CIRCUS ACT
Dancing poodle acts date back at least to 18th-century France, when trainers tapped into the water dog's intelligence and grace. José Olate continues the tradition with the touring UniverSoul Circus, based in Atlanta, Georgia. His standard poodle ballerinas tiptoe to music and execute back flips for urban audiences around the country.
Photo by Aristide Economopoulos,
The Star-Ledger

RELEASE THE HOUNDS
Although these foxhounds don't actually kill their prey—the 80-year-old Metamora Hunt Club has a rule against harming the foxes—Huntsman Pat Pearce and Master of Foxhounds Joe Kent still train the club's 60 dogs to nose out quarry that has gone to ground.
Photo by Steve Jessmore, The Flint Journal

GIT ALONG LITTLE DOGIE

Teaching Zucchini to ride, Avery Gauthier tries to dissuade the pup from settling down on the south end of the northbound pinto. Moments after this picture was taken, the agreeable dachshund and the patient pony were properly aligned—and moseyin' along.

Photo by Peter Goldberg

POWER PLAY

Misti, an Australian shepherd/border collie mix, sizes up a colt on Randy Billinger's Kansas ranch. Before the horses discover their own strength, Misti enjoys a brief period of dominance in the corral. "After about a year, though, the colts realize they can chase her back, and the tables turn," says Billinger.

Photo by Earl Richardson

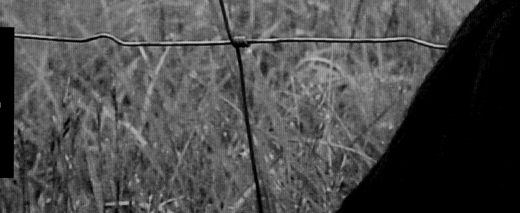

BORN TO HERD

Midge, a 3-year-old border collie, watches the action at a Kentucky stockdog competition. In previous centuries, stockdogs were essential for herding and guarding livestock. By the mid-20th century, however, the decline in predators and the decrease in range land put many out of work—but not these pros.
Photo by Dan Brandenburg

THE PROTECTORS

The vigilance of Akbash guard dogs is legendary: Often, females refuse to leave the flock to mate. Zoe (left) of Shepherd's Dairy Farm in Nebraska once decided a lamb was her puppy and denied the mother access. At the scent of a coyote, Toby (right) herds his flock to safer ground.
Photo by Bill Ganzel

TEAMWORK

During lambing season, Mike Curuchet keeps a close eye on his flock with the help of his three border collies, Cat, Duke, and Rebel. The dogs manage the movement of Curuchet's 1,950 sheep across 11,000 acres of Wyoming rangeland. "In my experience, they communicate about as well as humans," he says.

Photo by Bobby Model

CONTROL FREAK
Quill cuts four sheep out of the herd during Kentucky's annual Bluegrass Classic Open Stockdog Trial. The competition simulates farm chores: separating an injured animal, gathering sheep into the barn, or penning them. To be effective, the dog must have enough presence to instill respect in the sheep and enough "handler control" to steer them.
Photo by Ken Weaver

LEADING THE BLIND

At a suburban train station, trainers with the Fidelco Guide Dog Foundation acclimatize novice guide dogs to platforms, turnstiles, escalators, subway cars, and ticket booths. After six months of training, the German shepherds will become full-time assistants to blind adults in Boston and New York City.

Photo by Gerrit G. Bradley

SNOOP DOG

Bomb squad technician Ray Crowley and Spanky conduct planter patrol outside the Federal Building in downtown New Haven, Connecticut. Spanky, a 3-year-old golden retriever/yellow Lab mix, was recruited after 9/11, when bomb-sniffing dogs became a top priority for homeland security.

Photo by Peter Casolino

GOTCHA!

"I like the adrenaline," says steelworker Randal Skelton, explaining why he moonlights as a human chew toy. At a skills competition for German shepherds, 90-pound Odin attacks Skelton when he pops out from behind a blind during the "protection" test. "Odin bites especially hard," notes Skelton.

Photo by Bruce Strong, LightChasers

MAN'S BEST FRIEND

"It's really cool when a dog and a human can share equally in solving a problem," says handler Tim Hanavan of his relationship with Sam, a first responder with the nonprofit Chesapeake Search Dog team of Maryland. The golden retriever was one of the first dogs to search the Pentagon after the 9/11 attacks.

Photo by Herrmann + Starke

A SMILE IN THE AFTERNOON

Certified therapy dog Kippie elicits a moment of affection from Dorothy Wagner, 99, a resident of an Ohio rest home. With his tricks and cuddly nature, the little schipperke spends his time visiting patients in nursing homes and children's hospitals. "He loves people and couldn't care less about other dogs," says trainer Kim LeCompte.

Photo by Patrick Reddy, Cincinnati Enquirer

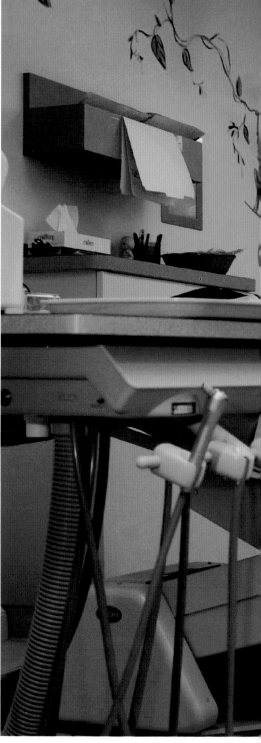

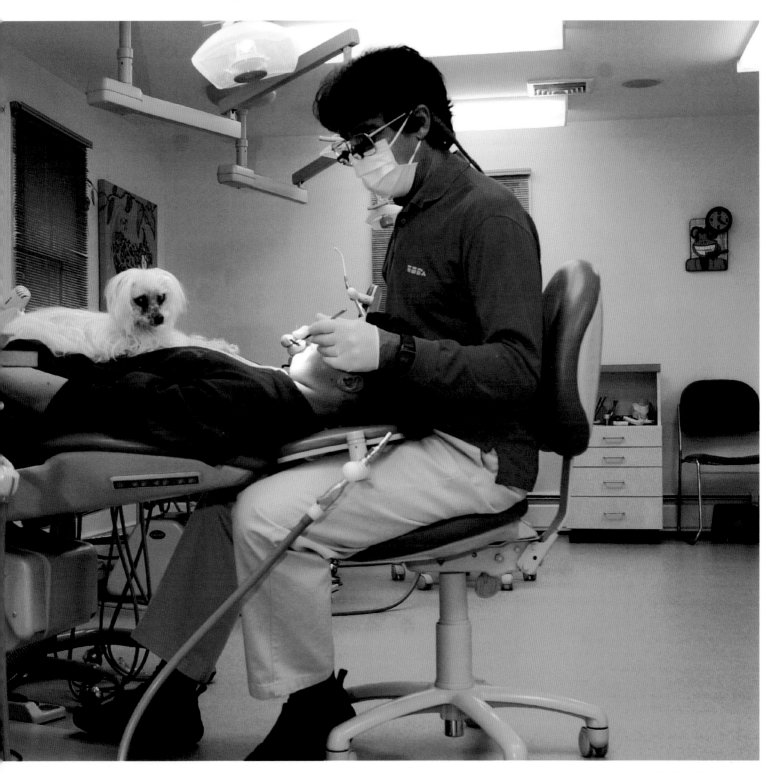

BEDSIDE MANNER

Silkie, a toy Maltese, diverts young patients while they get their teeth cleaned at a dental office in Marlborough, Massachusetts. The kids actually look forward to their appointments, knowing Silkie will be there.
Photo by Michele McDonald

A DAY AT THE RACES

Coveted by 11th-century English kings, the greyhound still draws admirers at Florida's Derby Lane dog track. Today, a purebred racer from a champion line can fetch $10,000. But the controversial sport doesn't always value the dogs, and an estimated 3,000 greyhounds are euthanized annually.

Photos by Beth Reynolds,
The Photo-Documentary Press, Inc.

BORN TO RUN

Running at 37 mph, greyhounds chase a stuffed-rabbit lure, controlled by this operator high above Derby Lane track. As fast as the sleek dogs are, these days the bleachers are rarely full. Over the past decade, bets wagered at U.S. dog tracks have declined 45 percent.

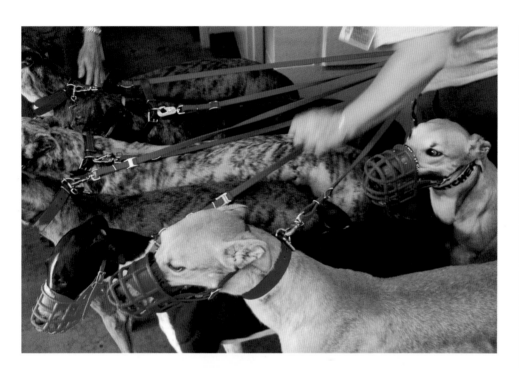

WATER DOG

On Sakonnet Bay in Rhode Island, Bella yanks on a cleated line aboard the fishing vessel *Maria Mendonsa.* "If you put anything in Bella's mouth, she'll pull it," says Bella's guardian, crewmember Luke Wheeler. At home, the Portuguese water dog helps with the yard work by ripping out runaway brambles.

Photos by Dave Hansen

BASS VS. PASTA
Surrounded by scup and bass, Bella begs for a taste of Wheeler's spaghetti. (She likes her fish cooked.) He regularly shares meals with Bella, especially when they're ashore.

RIDING SHOTGUN

During the 18th century, dalmatians guarded horse-drawn carriages from marauders. The dashing spotted hound was the only breed ever to serve this purpose. Three centuries later, 8-year-old Tito accompanies James Eskridge on his predawn trips into Chesapeake Bay to collect crab pots.

Photo by Vicki Cronis

HARBOR DOGS

While Labs are often used for hunting, guiding the blind, sniffing out drugs and mines, and retrieving fishnets, these two handsome specimens of America's most popular breed are content just surveying Waerwick, Rhode Island's, harbor from their clamming skiff.

Photo by Jason O'Neal

BASIC INSTINCT
At Kahle Meadow in Nevada, Zeke senses *something* in the reeds and immediately goes to point. The Hungarian vizsla made its way to North America when emigrants fled Hungary during World Wars I and II and took their prized hunting dogs with them.
Photo by Eric Jarvis

DOG DAY AFTERNOON At the annual Dog Swim Fest, pooches take over the pool in Eau Claire, Wisconsin. A $5 entrance fee supports an off-leash dog park. *Photo by Erika Hallberg*

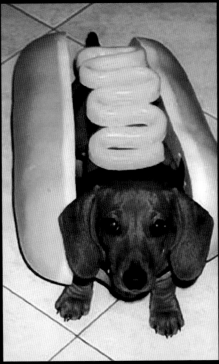

DACHSHUND DELIGHT Melvis hates this costume, but it does the trick for Halloween, netting the German hunting dog more treats than his human escorts ever get. *Photo by George Hamblen*

CHILLIN' The epitome of fashion, Oliver, a beagle-husky-hound mix, shows off his new Doggles in the backyard. *Photo by Gary Kelso*

WAVE CHASER *"He is my other eyes that can see above the clouds....He is the part of me that can reach out into the sea."* —Gene Hill, Author. ***Photo by John Johnsson***

BREATH OF FRESH AIR Pebble is usually too hyper to stand still, but after a morning workout along the Oregon coastline, the Yorkshire terrier stops for a breather and a smile.
Photo by Lan Luu

Who's the Lucky Dog?

Michael J. Rosen

The signs are everywhere. Bumper stickers that exclaim "Honk if You Love Vizslas!" or "I ♠ My Jack Russell" or "My Golden Retriever Is Smarter Than Your Honor Student." The mailbox offers more evidence: catalogues from exclusive purveyors of direct-to-you must-haves that you and your dog have thus far managed to live without: fluoridated chew toys, fire-engine-red toenail polish, dog-massage vibrators, Halloween costumes (Glenda, the Good-Dog Witch), *pet*igreed bottled water.

Lucky dogs have become even luckier in the past few decades. Does it make you wonder if they were previously unhappy? Were our pooches unfulfilled before Americans started spending some $34 billion annually on pet products? What does it really mean when the number of household cats and dogs is almost double the number of children in the United States?

Not long ago, a tennis ball and the occasional stick supplied 100 percent of a dog's daily toy requirement. And while the stick may have come in many outdoorsy flavors, the tennis ball came in one. Today, tennis balls possess a rainbow of flavors and electric colors, and dogs might actually start wondering where the rackets are.

Likewise, Jiffy Pop used to suffice as an unofficial dog treat, particularly after the Kraft singles had all disappeared into the lunch box. Now stores and catalogues offer more "homemade" treats than a church cookie-swap. Was canine interest in the same-old-same-old, bone-shaped biscuit trending downward? Had there been begging for more exotic victuals—and, more critically, had that been distinguishable from just regular begging? However it arose, we now have some dog people swearing by dried lamb-lung treats, while others insist on smoked pig tails. Households are stocking microwaveable

Woffy-Pop and Frosty Paws—a frozen confection that's twice as expensive as your scoop of Marshmallow Moosetracks—but it's vet-approved! Besides, isn't sharing your carb-loaded cone from the Dairy Queen just a little down-market?

Your mom-and-pop pet shop has been replaced with Smarty Pet Superstore Emporia Center, 24-Hour Clinic & Carpet Cleaning. Meanwhile, those boutiques—let's call them Too-Far-Gone to the Dogs—feature portrait galleries, stroller rentals for rainy dog walks, and catering departments specializing in doggie bar mitzvahs, birthdays, and coronations.

Animal testing has come full circle. We're now into human testing: couture, furnishings, jewelry, perfume—what's good enough for me is good enough for my dog. A dog trainer I know received a call from one of his more affluent clients who'd just picked up a tiny mink coat that she'd ordered for her King Charles spaniel...to match her own, of course. "As soon as I put it on Mitzi I had a horrible thought!" the lady told the trainer. "What if, on a walk, some other dog thinks she's a real mink and attacks her? Weren't some dogs bred to kill minks?" Could such a scenario have been imagined 50 years ago? We are a new breed, we dog owners.

A New Age pet-product catalogue features transformative tonics and environmental elixirs such as a pet aromatherapy kit with Pet Mist, Pet Massage Topical, Pet Synergy, and Pet Flower Essence. Our Labrador got such a catalogue in the mail because, for a time, we took out magazine subscriptions in our dogs' names in order to see who sold their mailing lists elsewhere. (As a result, our golden retriever was a member of the Democratic National Committee and our mixed breed was invited to have his own entry in *Who's Who in American Business*.)

The aromatherapy kit's sales copy began with a small reproach: "You know how much you enjoy the benefits of aromatherapy. Isn't it about time you let your pet in on this powerful secret?" While I have yet to enjoy such promised benefits, it was the word "secret" that threw me. I have no powerful—or any other type of—secret from my dogs, nor are my dogs preoccupied by anything that might be construed as a secret (such as the fact that there is *another* smoked turkey in the downstairs freezer).

When the kit arrived, the two dogs sniffed at the tubes and vials intended to enhance their "health, happiness, and environment." To be honest, they showed equal interest in the UPS truck that delivered the goods; its arrival triggers such blissful barking that I wondered how a bottled scent might ever rival it.

Nonetheless, I misted, dabbed, and rubbed the dogs as instructed. Nostrils widened, muzzles wrinkled, ears flattened—the same behavior they offer when I apply their flea preventative. I added the Pet Massage Topical to the usual stroking and petting they receive each day. I read the aromatherapy labels aloud: "Soyal oil, sunflower oil, organic..." Where was dead-fish oil? Is there a more essential oil for a dog's happiness? Where was the bouquet of squirrel tracks? Where was deer droppings, skillet drippings, or rabbit raisins? What could be more topical or therapeutic than smoke signals from the barbecue, which beckon the way the word "come" only works in theory?

Over subsequent days, I kept my eyes open for signs of an "enhanced environment"; alas, the environment remained house-like. As for the dogs' health and happiness, perhaps I didn't know what to look for. Or maybe adding another plus to the A+ they already assigned to their lives just didn't count for much.

Maybe New Age can't hold a candle—essential oil scented or not—to the Same-Old Age of canine contentment. No news is, in fact, dog news, and that's just the way animals (admit it: you're one) seem to like things. Who wouldn't trade the "newsworthy" for the plain old worthy?

Not only have we spent money and time customizing the lives of lucky dogs, we've customized dogs to suit the lives of unlucky people who once had legitimate reasons not to have a dog.

Parents concerned about allergies can't dismiss their child's request for a puppy anymore. "Sweetheart, if there were a dog here, Daddy wouldn't be able to breath, and you wouldn't want that, would you?" Now a child doesn't have to weigh the pros and cons. "Well, we can get a poodle, or a bishon, or Labradoodle, or...."

(Consumer News Alert: The so-called hypoallergic breeds now come with shed-resistant coats, making them a good fit for fastidious homeowners who, up till now, eschewed dogs because of the endless vacuuming. Sweep those concerns aside!)

This fickle dog fancying of ours has only just begun: Do you adore that jittery Italian greyhound who demands to be carried constantly but worry that your arms will get tired? Well, just for you, we might create a table-friendly, biscotti-sized greyhound you can feed from your espresso cup. Love that bug-eyed pug, but have you wondered if the dog's coat came in colors exclusively available to Chesapeake Bay retrievers? Watch for ads in a forthcoming issue of *Pugly Duckling*.

Travelers and people who work long hours have abundant options for their companions: puppy play centers, in-home pet care, certified dog walkers, and day spas featuring low-impact aerobics, hot tubbing, and dogudrama DVDs. America's new domestic policy is "take me, take my dog." AAA has listings for more than 12,000 hotels that cater to the 15 million of us who travel with pets. When my parents drove us bored brats across the states, "Are we there yet?" did not refer to a dog-friendly hotel. There were barely kid-friendly hotels then, unless you considered the lack of a lifeguard at the motel pool a sign of friendship. As for the family dog, what's the point of having neighbors?

Extra-lucky dogs at extra-fancy hotels are treated to VIP (Very Important Pet) amenity programs. Consider the Four Seasons in Boston, where my dogs and I were on assignment once for a travel magazine. Kibble and iced water, chews with the dogs' names scripted in icing, and cushy dog beds greeted us in our room. Once I concluded that exuberant tails could do no real damage to the room's appointments, we ordered everything from the chef's pet menu. A linen-draped cart arrived bearing silver-domed plates, starched placemats, and an orchid spray. While I hesitate to put the dogs' opinions into words, at $3 an entrée, I considered calling in another order for *my* lunch. The "Barnyard Chase," marked with an asterisk on the menu to signal that it was healthy alternative cuisine, consisted of freshly shucked corn and a chicken breast with grill marks branded at perfect right angles. Only an actual chase around the barnyard would have pleased the dogs more. "German Shepherd's Pie" consisted of velvety mashed potatoes piped around a ground beefsteak au jus. Au jus? Oh yes, the dogs chorus.

Does our divine indulgence know no bounds? Do they even notice this pampering? Isn't pleasing us their paradise?

As a guest on a Miami radio talk show, I took a call from an elderly listener who had a question about her miniature poodles. "One is a beautiful eater, but her sister—what am I going to do?—she won't eat unless I feed her with a special little spoon!"

"Tell her you lost the special spoon—you don't really have to lose it, just pretend," I suggested calmly, reasonably. "She'll soon start eating from a bowl."

Who isn't guilty of a little indulgence? Dogs are so amusing, how can you ignore, let alone scold, a family member who is making you laugh? Our adored golden retriever likes to make snow angels. After 30 or so seconds of flailing and squirming on the snow, Paris rises, shakes, and traipses over to the next activity. But there, burnished into a white drift, is a snow angel. The wings aren't really distinguishable from the body, and it's hard to tell whether the angel is right-side up or upside-down, but nonetheless, it is our dog's angelic, earth-bound impression.

Later in the day, the sun melts most of the yard's snow, all but the place where the warmth of Paris's body compressed and polished the snow into ice. His translucent white aura remains, glowing in the otherwise sodden and dingy lawn as though it were, in fact, a little miracle, a sighting to prove that something heavenly had lit there.

But then, come spring, Paris repeats that same creation—rolling on his back and clawing lawn rather than snow so that his paws de-thatch, uproot, and eventually score the soil as though we were about to sow grass seed. (Which we then need to do.) "No, you crazy angel, stop!" I command...and laugh, which Paris understands makes a double negative, and a reason to continue squirming in the grass.

Years from now, when Paris becomes that other kind of angel, I'll still believe in that sign, just as I'll believe that my golden retriever was smarter than most honor students. I want to believe in anything that reaffirms our love of this age-old, indulgent world— especially the miracles that dogs can bring us.

Are we the lucky dogs, or what?

Called "something of a fidosopher" by The Washington Post, *Michael J. Rosen is the author or editor of some 60 books for children and adults, including* Dog People: What We Love About Our Dogs *and* 21st Century Dog: A Visionary Compendium.

A Dog's Life

THE GOOD LIFE
Rocky, a 9-year-old yellow Lab, seeks the shade after a long afternoon chasing baitfish near Marvin Key, Florida.
Photo by Rob O'Neal

BOING, BOING, BOING!
"Take the frog for a leap," Gary Porter tells his grandkids Mason, 6, and Melena Steffes, 7, when his Jack Russell terrier needs a walk. Trixie's levitations—she's been known to hit 3 feet—are so well-known that neighbors drop what they're doing to watch her go by.
Photo by Gary W. Porter

GRAVY TRAIN
Daisy gets a ride around St. Michael's Convent on Reverend Mother Mary Katrina's cart. The hound mix spends her days taking walks with the sisters, waiting outside the chapel, and playing in her fenced yard. "If she gets out," says Sister Mary Katrina, "she'll find the dirtiest, smelliest patch possible and let us all know about it."
Photo by Torsten Kjellstrand

WHO BROUGHT THE CARDS?
After an evening obedience class, trainer Celeste Meade briefs Breaker, Zipper, and Zoom on the dessert specials at a training and boarding facility in New Hampshire. Meade has trained the dogs to sit at the table when called.
Photo by Bob Hammerstrom

MUTTLEY CREW

Walking up to 10 dogs at a time takes some strength, according to professional dog walker Stuart Parsons, shown here with seven charges passing the legendary Dakota Apartments on Manhattan's Central Park West. "If they spot a squirrel, you're going for a ride."

Photo by Martha Cooper

URBAN MUSHER

Jennifer Wood-Czuprynski gathers speed on her mutt-powered scooter in Bay City, Michigan. Czisa, a dalmatian/poodle mix, isn't exactly Iditarod material—she lasts only a few blocks on the towline before she gets tired.
Photo by Kent Miller, The Bay City Times

WIENER WORLD

Romping through the woods along the Grand Canyon's East Rim is a daily pleasure for 7-year-old Alexandra Simon; her dachshunds, Abu, Glover, and Peaches; and her dad, Starbuck, a shopping center manager.
Photo by Christine Keith

NANOOK OF THE MIDWEST

Skyler Parsons, 5, puts his American Eskimo, Nanook, through his acrobatic paces. Called American spitzes until World War I when German words became taboo, the circus dog is known for its agility and easy traveling manner.
Photo by Don Parsons

VERTICALLY CHALLENGED
Squirrels torment 4-year-old Chance, a stray mutt found by Michael Woods in a machine shop parking lot one Christmas Eve. He spends most days chasing rodents along the backyard fence and up tree trunks like this one near Buck Creek Lake in Ohio. Says Woods, "He's never caught one." Yet.
Photo by Bill Reinke, Dayton Daily News

ALLEY OOP!
Doing sideways jumps over Rene Bruce's leg is just one of Kia's moves. The 2-year-old Jack Russell terrier models, surfs, kayaks, mountain bikes, inner tubes, rides Harleys with Bruce—and has her own website. "Skydiving is next on our list," Bruce says.
Photo by Shelly Castellano, www.SCPIX.com

DOWNWARD DOG
Pokey is not a high-culture creature. The fox terrier is unimpressed when Chris Bennett, Jr. begins his violin lesson with teacher Sammy Carruthers in Bentonsport, Iowa. Indeed, the 9-year-old's halting rendition of Beethoven's "Ode to Joy" is Pokey's signal to take a nap.
Photo by John Gaines, The Hawk Eye

HOT DOG

Lasne, a 7-month-old Hungarian komondor puppy, stops for refreshment on a humid afternoon. The komondor, bred to guard sheep, has a thick white coat that felts and cords like sheep's wool. The disguise would surprise marauding bears and wolves—beasts Lasne is unlikely to encounter in the Florida suburbs.
Photo by Brian Fogarty

GOING TO THE DOGS

"I thought working with dogs might be more interesting than working with people," says Marie Emery, explaining why she left her job at Boeing to start Best Friends Dogwalking. "And I was right." Emery spends her mornings at Blue Dog Pond's off-leash area, one of nine such facilities in Seattle.
Photo by Alan Berner

ISLAND DUFFERS

Twelve-year-old Sammy, attached to the U.S. Coast Guard since birth, has had his share of knocks during his years stationed on Little Brewster Island in Boston Harbor. The Lab broke several ribs tumbling down the lighthouse stairwell and nearly fell overboard during an evacuation in the middle of a nor'easter. "But really," says Assistant Lightkeeper Ben O'Brien, "he's a happy dog."
Photo by Laurie Swope

DOGS ON THE BUS
To be admitted to the Common Dog Bed & Breakfast club, Boston-area canines must pass a sociability screening. If they're judged worthy, the day care center sends a van to bring them in.
Photo by Arthur Pollock, Boston Herald

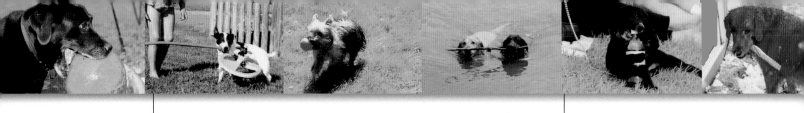

PUP VS. KID

Ashley Dunkin and her neighbor's dog Gidget battle for control of the family sprinkler. As soon as Ashley gets close enough to cool off, the pesky pup snatches the hose and takes off running. After a long chase, Gidget finally surrenders. Dog 2, Toddler 1.

Photo by Paul Rutherford

COCO-COLA

The soft mouth of the Labrador makes it a great game retriever, but teething 12-week-old Coco prefers to rip into a Diet Coke bottle.

Photo by Rob Carr

PUPPY LOVE

The Nye family's new puppy, Twozee, chews some shoe during an evening Little League game in Manchester, New Hampshire.

Photo by Don Himsel, The Telegraph

NO, IT'S MINE!

A rubber disk is Dakhota's reward for completing a scent-tracking exercise. A golden retriever's sophisticated nose detects airborne skin cells, sweat, and body oils—a sensitivity that has made Dakhota an invaluable member of the Kentucky Search Dog Association, which responds to emergencies in eastern Kentucky.

Photo by Janet Worne, Lexington Herald-Leader

TO EACH HIS OWN
In Charlie's view of things, golden retriever Beesley is a hyperactive simpleton. The 11-year-old shih tzu just watches while his roommate starts in with the fetching and running-in-circles routine.
Photo by Kevin Eilbeck

FREE-RANGE DOG
Open space is a rare gift in New York City. Racing around the 86th Street dog run, these boys take full advantage of their hour of freedom.
Photo by Barbara Alper

GO FOR THE GOAL

Once all the rage, rough collies have declined in popularity since the final episode of *Lassie* aired in 1971. Unlike her namesake, this Lassie rarely wanders farther than her soccer ball can be thrown—and has never rescued anyone from a well.
Photo by Lisa Rudy Hoke

RESERVOIR DOG

Drake trains at a reservoir in Kansas, where diving for quail dummies takes a keen eye and a soft mouth. Ancestors of the aquatically inclined Labrador retriever were first employed by Newfoundland fisherman in the 16th century to retrieve cork floats and fishing nets. Recreational hunter Kip Etter hones Drake's inherited skills daily.
Photo by Kelly Glasscock

ON THE FLY
Carolynn Williams throws a Frisbee for her Australian shepherd, Rafe, during a Humane Society event in Frederick, Maryland. The two are warming up for the SkyHoundz Hyperflite championship later that day.
Photo by Perry Thorsvik

LAB SCIENCE
When Labradors like 2-year-old Delia engage in retrieving, they undergo a physiologic transformation. Body temperatures rise, blood carbon dioxide levels drop, and metabolic acid increases as they become monomaniacal fetching machines.
Photo by John Gurzinski

FOR THE FUN OF IT

Kika loves nothing better than to hang out on Lake Tahoe's Nevada Beach. His favorite sport? Catching sand. When someone throws a handful, the Hungarian vizsla leaps, sometimes 5 feet straight up.

Photo by Eric Jarvis

Love Is Never Having to Say Anything at All

By Patricia B. McConnell

Photo by Patrick Reddy, Cincinnati Enquirer

Cool Hand Luke is not going to die. I won't stand for it. I know, of course, that he will, at least a part of me does.

After all, he's 11, he's a dog, and he's already cheated death from cancer, cars, and a 300-pound ram determined to kill him or me, whoever came first. I'm more grateful than I can say that Luke is still here. His front paws may be swollen with arthritis and he may tire easily, but he still loves working sheep, fetching tennis balls, and sitting in silence with me in the rosy light of the sunset. And I still love him so completely that I imagine his death to be as if all the oxygen in the air disappeared, and I was left to try to survive without it.

I'm not alone in this love affair. Everywhere I go I talk to people who have soul mates like Luke, dogs so special we get tears in our eyes just talking about them. This phenomenon is not new—people have been in love with their dogs for centuries. Nor is the love of pets unique to industrial societies—even hunter/gatherer societies have animal companions.

While not everyone loves dogs, there's a phenomenon that needs explaining: Those of us who love dogs love them so deeply it hurts. It's easy to demean these feelings, as people often do. Dog lovers have been described as neurotics or social incompetents, and though dog lovers can be just as emotionally illiterate as the rest of the world, loving dogs is not, in itself, the problem. There's something much bigger than neediness that drives our love of dogs. People the world over have sought an answer to why we love dogs, perhaps an indication that the question is deeply rooted. I don't think it's a trivial question, either, and not just because I'm stupid in love with my dogs. I'm also a scientist and applied animal behaviorist, and from the perspective of biology, the question is both interesting and important.

Indeed, biology itself provides some of the answers. One obvious connection between dogs and humans is our shared natural history. Dogs and people may be strikingly different in many ways, but, if you compare our behavior with that of other animals, we share more than we don't. Like dogs, people sleep, eat, and hunt together, and that in itself is notable in the animal kingdom. Pandas are notoriously solitary. Feral cats can live in groups or alone, but they don't hunt together. Butterflies are often seen together, but only because they're attracted to the same minerals in the puddle in your driveway. In contrast to animals who are seen together without social relationships, dogs and humans are so social that we even raise our young together, sometimes deferring our own reproduction in order to assist another member of the group. Individuals of both species will nurse the young of another female, and that fact alone puts dogs and humans in a special category.

Many other factors of our natural history have a profound effect on our relationship with dogs. Dogs, like people, live in social hierarchies, and are generally amenable to doing what high-status individuals ask of them. Both human beings and dogs are "Peter Pan animals," whose behavior is shaped by a process called paedomorphism, in which adult, sexually mature individuals retain the characteristics of adolescents, remaining curious and playful all their lives. It's easy to take playing with your dog for granted, but go ask a cow to play with you and see how far you get.

Equally important is our shared tendency to nurture needy individuals. In both species, offspring are born helpless, desperately in need of care and a safe environment in which to learn survival skills. Humans have such an extended period of parental care that we're hard-wired to go weak-kneed at animals who look infantile. If you want people to feel all warm and gooey and nurturing, show them a baby mammal with a disproportionately large forehead and oversized hands, and listen for the "Awww's" coming out of the crowd. This reaction to young, needy mammals is such a primal part of who we are that psychologists have labeled it the "Aw phenomenon."

Dogs don't stay cute little puppies for long, but they remain dependent and nonverbal, much like very young children. Some of us may have great respect for our dogs, as I do for Luke, but, although he can load the ram on the truck single-handedly, he still can't open doors or pull his dinner out from that magic place under the counter. Natural selection has emphasized nurturance in our species, and surely dogs have profited from it.

All these shared characteristics are important, but somehow all of them don't seem enough to explain the passion many of us have for our dogs. A love of play and strategic hunting techniques may drive our relationship, but a shared natural history isn't enough of an explanation when some big, strong fireman is sobbing in my office while discussing euthanizing his dog. The depth of pain we dog lovers feel when facing the loss of one of our best friends can be overwhelming.

In some ways it's similar to the grief we feel when we lose a human loved one. But something not particularly obvious is different about our grief over losing a dog: People who've never cried in their lives cry over losing their dogs. I'll never forget the episode of the TV series *M*A*S*H* when, surrounded by the relentless agonies of injured and dying soldiers in Korea, the medical team coped with black humor, bravery, and stamina—until a little stray dog they'd adopted died. Then they fell apart. It may have been just a television show, but it reflected something universally true about the effect dogs have on us.

I remember watching the movie *My Dog Skip* with a friend and crying at the end with the same pure emotion I saw on that *M*A*S*H* episode. We weren't simply crying about the loss of a dog, we were crying over loss itself, and, when personified in a dog, that sense of loss was easier to let out. The tendency of humans to be able to grieve so deeply over a dog indicates that something big and primal and important goes on between people and dogs that has as much to do with our emotions as our shared natural history.

So why is it, then, that dogs can elicit the purity of emotion we often cover up in our human relationships? Perhaps, just perhaps, it is because dogs don't talk. Sure, you already knew that. But the more I think about the consequences of our nonverbal relationship with dogs, the more benefits there are. Psychologists have told us for years that dogs give us "nonjudgmental positive regard," and we intuitively understand exactly what that means. The pure and simple joy that radiates from our dogs every time we come home is rarely duplicated in human greetings, and it can elicit the feeling of pure love that we all seek from infancy onward. Dogs indeed love us with tremendous intensity, and the fact that they can't talk acts to underscore it, not diminish it.

Of course we can communicate with dogs. They understand hundreds of the words we use and get a tremendous amount of information from our intonation. But even the most avid dog lover can't sit down and have an in-depth conversation with their dog.

If dogs could talk, I suspect things wouldn't feel so pure and simple. Though most of our dogs love us deeply, they don't necessarily love us every second of the day. Luke can shoot me a look that can be summed up in two words. The second is "you," but the first is not "love." Why should intelligent individuals not make judgments about what happens to them? Surely our dogs can get frustrated if we delay that walk in the woods for the phone call that came just as we were going out the door, just like our spouses or partners can. I don't say this cynically, and I don't want to burst any sacred bubbles, but perhaps what dogs give us is the *perception* of continual "nonjudgmental positive regard." If I could teach Luke to talk, I'm not sure I'd always be happy about what he had to say.

A hurtful word can live a long time in the heart of the receiver, and influence the relationship forever after. In the case of dogs, perhaps it's easier to ignore an irritation here and a ruffled feather there, because our dogs can't put words to them. "Sticks and stones may break my bones but words will never hurt me" may be a common refrain, but it's not based in reality. Words can cause terrible damage, sometimes lasting a lifetime, and the fact that dogs can't use them may be a blessing.

Our lack of a shared language can be a great disadvantage, causing us grief when we're desperate to ask our dogs what's wrong, or yearning to explain why we're torturing them with another radiation treatment. Our ability to talk to one another may be one of the greatest accomplishments of the human species, and there are times when I'd give anything to be able to communicate with Luke in greater depth than I can now. But speech comes with a price. Being in conversation with even a good friend raises your blood pressure. It takes a lot of mental energy to make decisions about what words to say, how to string them together, what tone to use when you say them. That's the very same energy that spiritual leaders advise us to turn off as a way of revitalizing ourselves. The constant conversation that most of us have in our heads can be exhausting and is so inherent to the way our brains work that we actually have to practice turning it off. Anyone who's tried meditation knows how difficult it can be to shut off the internal chatter that comes with being verbal.

Experts at meditation can be "in the present," and free of mental noise for hours, but I'm thrilled to turn off my brain for just a minute or two. That's because I'm a novice at a skill we humans need to learn and practice. But I doubt Luke has to practice meditating to be able to experience the kind of spiritual peace humans have to learn to find. Being nonverbal allows an otherwise intelligent, highly connected animal to live in the present without the hailstorm of internal conversations that complicate our human lives. If you think about it, most of what we "talk" about in our own heads isn't about the present, it's about the past or future. But dogs keep us firmly rooted in the here and now, and that, it turns out, is a notable accomplishment.

Where but with dogs can we have such a deep and meaningful relationship with so little baggage? Words may be wonderful things, but they carry weight with them, and there's a great lightness of being when they are discarded. The story of the Garden of Eden is a lovely allegory about the cost of cognition. Being able to use our brains the way we do separates us from the rest of the animal world, and, like most everything else in life, it has its costs as well as its benefits.

Perhaps it's not just the things we share with dogs that wrap us together in mutual love. In the lovely, balanced irony of yin and yang, it's the differences as much as the similarities that bring us together. Some of my happiest times are when Luke and I sit silently together, overlooking the green, rolling hills of southern Wisconsin. Our lack of language doesn't get in the way, but creates an opening for something else, something deep and pure and good. We dog lovers share a Zen-like communion with our dogs, uncluttered by nouns and adverbs and dangling participles. This connection speaks to a part of us that needs to be nurtured and listened to, but is so often drowned out in the cacophony of speech. Dogs remind us that we are being heard, without the additional weight of words. What a gift. No wonder we love them so much.

The author of The Other End of the Leash: Why We Do What We Do Around Dogs, *Patricia B. McConnell, PhD, is a certified applied animal behaviorist who teaches at the University of Wisconsin-Madison.*

Mug Shots

STREET TOUGHS
Scout and Norman guard their turf on the 1100 block of Broadway in Manhattan. In the late 19th century, French bulldogs were fashionable companions in bohemian Paris. But as they fell out of style the breed's numbers dwindled. Scarcity increased their market value, and Frenchies now retail for up to $2,000 per pup.
Photo by Lou Manna, Olympus Camedia Master

STAR POWER
Daisy the dalmatian is between gigs as a therapy dog. It's a role that has patients cheering at hospitals in Fort Lauderdale, Florida. But wait, there's more: Daisy is an actress who has appeared in a beer commercial and is a card-carrying member of the Screen Actors Guild.
Photo by Lori Bale

THERAPY DOG

THE COMPANION

Balancing on rocks, swimming in icy rivers, skidding across frozen lakes, or mucking about in springtime fields—9-year-old Piper would do just about anything to keep up with her companion, sportsman Robert Aiken.

Photo by Jamie Gemmiti, Cross Road Studio

DUCK-CRAZY

Paddling with Starlight in upstate New York is a quiet pleasure for photographer Nancie Battaglia, unless the 46-pound springer spaniel detects a duck. Lickedy-split, Starlight will jump out of the canoe in pursuit, soaking her canoe-mate in the process. "She always adds some excitement to the day," says Battaglia fondly.

Photo by Nancie Battaglia

SCOTTIES ON WHEELS

Photographer Ruth Wynne's favorite subjects are her Scottish terriers Seamus, Molly, Angus, Brewster, and Megan. Wynne often poses the pack in their Halloween, back-to-school, and *Scot's Illustrated* swimsuit costumes.

Photo by Ruth M. Wynne

TAILGATING

A posse of Norfolk terriers—15-year-old patriarch, Ralph (rear), his consort Hana (second from right), and young'uns Reggie, Rex, Rosie, and Ruby—listen to Mel Goldman's instructions before they're allowed to exit the Volvo and run around the dog park.
Photo by Pamela Einarsen

ON THE FENCE

Nala was a gift to Arielle Hickel on her sixth birthday. "I named her after the girl lion from *The Lion King*, because she was cute and fluffy," says Arielle. The 1-year-old Akita spends a lot of time hanging on the backyard fence greeting passersby in the busy neighborhood.
Photo by Stacey Cramp

THE LONG GOODBYE

Karen Klitz embraces Max, her 12-year-old schnauzer, who suffers from a fatal liver disease. Most of all, Klitz says, she will miss Max's mischievous streak, which once led him to pull corncobs out of the trash and stash them in closets throughout the house.
Photo by Steve Bly, Bly Photography

PUGNATIOUS

Businessman Ben Friedman started Chicago's Pug Crawl in 1994 after throwing a birthday party for his beloved Knuckles. When six pugs showed up, he wondered just how many he could get together. In 2004, about 500 attended.
Photo by Maria Schriber

ENOUGH ALREADY!

It had been storming for weeks, and Beignet, a 9-year-old Catahoula Leopard dog, was noticeably grumpy. She had been kept inside and away from the neighborhood park.
Photo by C. Paige Burchel

GILDING THE LILY

Maryanne Martin likes Dipper's hot pink nail polish, but her son Jonathan prefers buttercup yellow. Dipper, a 1-year-old miniature poodle, goes to Abilene's Dog Gone Pretty Styling Salon and Petography Studio twice a month, once for a shampoo and once for a coif and pawdicure.
Photo by Ronald W. Erdrich,
Abilene Reporter-News

MINI ME

Two-year-old Lionel is a forbearing pup. Not only
is he tolerant of Ali Simpson's scary handbag,
but he patiently bides his time while she mingles
at an art gallery opening.
Photo by Peter Gemei

SHAMPOOCH

Louie gets the works—shampoo, rinse, and flea treatment—at Wags-N-Whiskers grooming salon. Pets like Louie fuel the $32 billion pet-grooming industry, which is expected to expand by 12 percent over the next five years.

Photos by Jeanie Adams-Smith
Western Kentucky University

JUST A LITTLE OFF THE TOP

Drizzit feels half his 27-pound weight after
Kim Doolin of Wags-N-Whiskers takes a
little—okay, a lot—off the top.

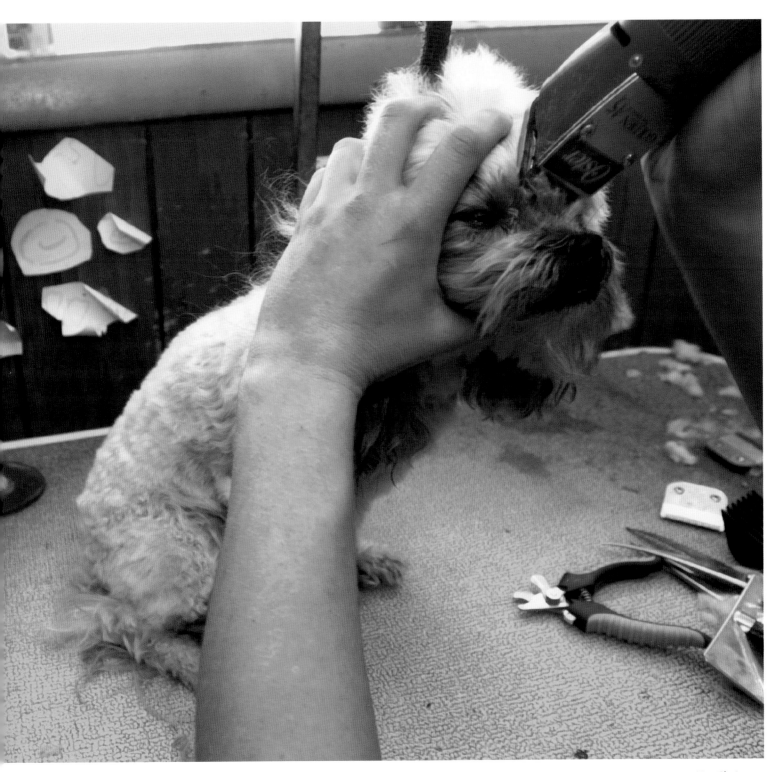

LONG AND SHORT OF IT
Tess, a Yorkshire terrier, runs with the big boys.
Her friend Blue, a German shepherd, trains with
her and several dozen other pals at an Ogden,
Utah, obedience club.
Photo by Leah Hogsten

YIN & YANG

Kelly, a typical Weimaraner, is a bundle of con-
tradictions: She's inquisitive yet timid, gentle
yet fearless. And, as far as guardian Denny
Carr can tell, the 3-year-old is just as happy
running alongside his bicycle on 10-mile treks
through the Sonoran desert as she is dozing in
the shade of her backyard palms.

Photo by Denny Carr, www.azimagery.com

BEAST OF BURDEN

An adventurer like her Wyoming outlaw name-sake, Cattle Kate pulls tourists through the snowbound meadows of the Bridger-Teton National Forest. In the summers, the husky stays in shape by towing ATVs around with her sledmates.

Photo by W. Garth Dowling

PILLOW TALK

Called the "pillow dog" in the 19th century, Chihuahuas are partial to padded seats and laps. Not one to stray far from convention, 8-year-old Simon spends his days in one of three places: Robert Brown's wheelchair, Cindy Brown's office swivel seat, or, his favorite, this generously stuffed and otherwise unclaimed armchair.

Photo by Mat Thorne,
Western Kentucky University

STICKING TOGETHER

Stick, toy, bone, Frisbee, you name it—if Zoey has it, Buddy wants it. The siblings compete over just about everything, but the rivalry is friendly and the Springer spaniels are, underneath it all, each other's closest allies.

Photo by Steve Harrington

DOG TIRED
Shyla, an 8-year-old yellow Lab, melts into her favorite love seat after an afternoon bounding through native prairie grasses in search of pheasant dummies, training for the next hunt.
Photo by Jeff Storjohann

About Our Sponsors

PURINA
Your Pet, Our Passion.™

WEBSHOTS

Lexar™

Nestlé Purina PetCare Company is proud to sponsor *Dogs 24/7* and *Cats 24/7*, two pictorial testaments to the wonderful role that dogs and cats play in our daily lives. As a leader in the pet products industry, Nestlé Purina PetCare Company is dedicated to improving the lives of dogs and cats through quality nutrition and care. Our core philosophies include promoting responsible pet care, humane education, community involvement, and the positive bond between people and their pets.

In addition to *Dogs 24/7* and *Cats 24/7*, Nestlé Purina is a proud supporter of the American Humane Association. Through programs such as "Very Best Pet Network" and "Pets for People," Nestlé Purina promotes pet adoptions and donates funds and pet food to animal shelters across America. Nestlé Purina also partners with a number of registries and organizations, including the Cat Fancier's Association (CFA), the International Kennel Club (IKC), the American Kennel Club (AKC), and the United Kennel Club (UKC), to support canine and feline enthusiasts at hundreds of dog and cat shows around the country. Nestlé Purina provides strong support to the AKC Canine Health Foundation to advance canine genetics and health.

The Purina Pet Institute is a multidisciplinary initiative that encompasses Nestlé Purina's Research and Development capabilities, alliances formed with pet care experts across the country, and the Healthy Pets 21 Consortium, a think tank of some of the foremost leaders in pet health and welfare. Healthy Pets 21 focuses on improving pet health and well-being and fostering the quality of pet owners' relationships with their pets. Its goals include promoting responsible pet ownership; raising awareness of issues and advances in pet health, behavior, and well-being; communicating the benefits of the human-pet relationship; and promoting a more pet-friendly society. Nestlé Purina also helps pets live long, healthy, and happy lives through advanced pet nutrition and care studies. At our pet nutrition and care centers in St. Joseph and Gray Summit, Missouri, we conduct studies that contribute to understanding the nutritional needs and feeding requirements of pets. Each year, Purina Dog Chow hosts Incredible Dog Challenge events across the country, culminating in the national championships at the 10-acre Canine Competition Center at Purina Farms. In these competitions, dogs demonstrate their remarkable skills as they strive for the title.

Nestlé Purina offers more than two dozen online Web sites that provide valuable information on responsible pet care, nutrition, and behavior, including Q & A's from veterinary experts, pet health and nutrition news, and fun promotional offers. You can reach all of our Web sites via:
www.purina.com
www.cats24-7.com/purina
www.dogs24-7.com/purina

Webshots is proud to be the official online photo site for *Dogs 24/7* and *Cats 24/7*.

We were eager to use our photo expertise and streamlined technology to power the online photo submission process and introduce our huge community of photo enthusiasts to this exciting new book program. The Pets category of shared photos on Webshots is an extremely popular destination with members viewing over 100,000 dog and cat photos every day.

Webshots, one of the world's largest photo sharing sites, provides consumers with a variety of ways to enjoy and share photos on their computer desktops, TVs, and mobile phones. Only Webshots enables its members to share photos with family and friends through unique features like Photo Messages ™, moblogging, online photo albums, and custom prints and gifts. And only Webshots offers free photo downloads from thousands of professional photos in our Gallery and millions of photos shared by Webshots members in our Community. Wildly popular, Webshots has millions of members who are passionate about their ability to browse the world's largest photo network and use the Web's best photo search.

Webshots, a CNET Networks company, was founded in 1995 and is based in San Francisco, California.

We encourage pet-loving photo enthusiasts everywhere to enjoy the beautiful photos in the *Dogs 24/7* and *Cats 24/7* book series—again and again—and to continue sharing their latest pictures of Fido and Fluffy online all year-round.

Lexar Media has grown from the digital photography revolution, which is why we are proud to have supplied the digital memory cards used in the *America 24/7* series. Lexar Media's high-performance memory cards utilize our unique and patented controller coupled with high-speed flash memory from Samsung, the world's largest flash memory supplier. This powerful combination brings out the ultimate performance of any digital camera.

Photographers who demand the most from their equipment choose our products for their advanced features like write speeds up to 40x, Write Acceleration technology for enabled cameras, and Image Rescue, which recovers previously deleted or lost images. Leading camera manufacturers bundle Lexar Media digital memory cards with their cameras because they value its performance and reliability.

Lexar Media is at the forefront of digital photography as it transforms picture-taking worldwide, and we will continue to be a leader with new and innovative solutions for professionals and amateurs alike.

Special thanks to Olympus, CNET, Digital Pond, Acronym, AOL, Reader's Digest, Dogster, Preclick, LaCie, Kompolt Online Auction Agency, and WebSideStory

Adobe

The *America 24/7* series gave digital photographers of all levels the opportunity to share their visions of what it means to live in the United States. This series was made possible by a digital photography revolution that is dramatically changing and improving picture-taking for professionals and amateurs alike. And an Adobe product, Photoshop®, has been at the center of this sea of change.

Adobe's products reflect our customers' passion for the creative process, be it the photographer, graphic designer, layout artist, or printer. Adobe is the Publishing and Imaging Software Partner for the *America 24/7* series and products such as Adobe InDesign®, Photoshop®, Acrobat®, and Illustrator® were used to produce this stunning book in a matter of weeks. We hope that our software has helped do justice to the mythic images, contributed by well-known photographers and the inspired hobbyist.

Adobe is proud to be a lead sponsor of the *America 24/7* series, a project that celebrates the vibrancy of the American spirit: the same spirit that helped found Adobe and inspires our employees and customers to deliver the very best.

Bruce Chizen
President and CEO
Adobe Systems Incorporated

Google's mission is to organize the world's information and make it universally accessible and useful.

With our focus on plucking just the right answer from an ocean of data, we were naturally drawn to the *America 24/7* series. The book you hold is a compendium of images of life distilled from thousands of photographs and infinite possibilities. Are you looking for emotion? Narrative? Shadows? Light? It's all here, thanks to a multitude of photographers and writers creating links between you, the reader, and a sea of wonderful stories. We celebrate the connections that constitute the human experience and are pleased to help engender them. And we're pleased to have been a small part of this project, which captures the results of that interaction so vividly, so dynamically, and so dramatically.

The founding promise of Mirra, Inc. is to help people protect and access their digital photos and files on their PCs with simple solutions that anyone can use, at any time and anywhere. We provide digital peace of mind so you never have to worry about losing life's irreplaceable moments—like family photos and the precious photos in *Dogs 24/7* and *Cats 24/7*. Thus we are delighted to be a sponsor for the 24/7 series. The Mirra Personal Server has made it possible for the editors of these 24/7 books to automatically and continuously protect, back up, and, when appropriate, share 24/7 photos via the Web—including hundreds of photos you see in these books. Kudos to *Dogs 24/7* and *Cats 24/7* for remembering that pets are family, too.

the dog culture magazine

Bark magazine is the voice of today's dog culture, exploring the special bond between dogs and humans. As the leading chronicler of life with dogs, *Bark* is pleased to be a sponsor of the *Dogs 24/7* project. We are proud to take part in this extraordinary celebration of dogs and the vibrant communities in which they live.

Bark shares the great passion America has for dogs, and delights in the many ways they contribute to our world as our faithful companions going back through the millennia. Our award-winning magazine—noted for its entertaining mix of stories and commentary, humor and poignancy, instruction and inspiration—touches all aspects of what we've come to know as the modern dog culture.

Bark, which began in a dog park in 1997, connects with dog people around the world. *Time* magazine deemed us "the *New Yorker* for dog lovers" and *Esquire* hailed us as the "coolest dog magazine ever." Four times a year, we share with our readers the joys and excitement of the world's oldest friendship. Our motto—Dog is my co-pilot—says it all. Subscriptions available at www.thebark.com.

AIRWAYS®

JetBlue Airways is proud to be the *America 24/7* series preferred carrier, flying photographers, photo editors, and organizers across the United States.

Winner of *Condé Nast Traveler*'s Readers' Choice Awards for Best Domestic Airline 2002, JetBlue provides friendly service and low fares for travelers in 22 cities in 9 states across America.

On behalf of JetBlue's 5,000 crew members, we're excited to be involved in this remarkable project, and for the opportunity to serve American travelers each and every day, coast to coast, 24/7.

Founded in 1995, eBay created a powerful platform for the sale of goods and services by a passionate community of individuals and businesses. On any given day, there are millions of items across thousands of categories for sale on eBay. eBay enables trade on a local, national, and international basis with customized sites in markets around the world.

Through an array of services, such as its payment solution provider PayPal, eBay is enabling global e-commerce for an ever-growing online community.

Thumbnail Picture Credits

Credits for thumbnail photographs are listed by the page number and are in order from left to right.

22 Wayne Seward
Sandra McGonigle
Ted Richardson,
   Winston-Salem Journal
Ann Vanlandingham
Gwen Young
Sue Conklin

23 Sara Hayden
Barbara Alper
Christine Gilpin
Bob Hornsby
Lloyd E. Jones,
   The Conway Daily Sun
Andrea Grapek

28 Les Ginn
Perry Thorsvik
Donna Tweed
Daniel Donovan
Michael Harp
Beth Potter

32 Vincent DeWitt,
   Cape Cod Times
Stacie Lynch
William H. Mullins
Charles Kimbrough
Tammy Ljungblad
Jack Sterling

38 Lisa Reinhardt
Stuart Brumbaugh
William K. Daby
Diane Dempsey Murray
Karen Brewer
Lee Tibbo

39 Denis Langlois
Pam Christiansen
Jim Laurie,
   Stephens Press
Amanda Loguidice
Donna Meier
Elise O'Keefe

40 Pierre Belhumeur
Peter Ackerman,
   Asbury Park Press
Angela Wrenn
Francine Dory
Trevor Brown, Jr.,
   Rich Clarkson & Associates
Shirley Jones

42 Lisa Riner
Gloria Smith
John Isaac
Maria Lee-Muramoto
Connie Hansen
Robin Anderson

43 Gabriela Thiel
John Freidah
Paula Michaels
Todd Stellges
Louise Shanley
Mark Carder

44 Wendy Heye
José Azel, Aurora
Lisa Riner
Rob Richman
Jim Lavrakas,
   Anchorage Daily News
Sandra Arias

45 Jaana Makkonen
Jolana Malatkova
Steve Marsman
Kane Schaller
Craig Fritz
Shaune Grose

58 Brenda Baldwin
Marlene Collins
Sheri Lehn
Rikki Ward
Charlie Lu
Denise Brewer

59 Beth Nash
Emma Kluger
Brenda DeWaele
Ligia Besser
James D. Smith
Whitney Hand

61 Barbara Kirby
Tiffany Sellers
W. Garth Dowling
Kim McCollum
Jeanie Adams-Smith,
   Western Kentucky University
Eurico Correia

62 Kristine McNamara
Les Marczi
Pamilyn Sanders
Philip Barr,
   The Birmingham News
Debbie Leech
Joe Simon

63 Wendy Bender
Joel Stuthman
John Lu
Penelope Williamson
Carrie Caldwell
Crystal Gomez

64 April Patterson
Jonathan Newton
Lise Templin
Aerin Green
Trevor Brown, Jr.,
   Rich Clarkson & Associates
Bruce Marsili

67 Katariina Sutphin
Lexey Swall,
   Naples Daily News
Terri LaGrippo
Tina Surjadi
Dee Marvin
David Simeral

72 Rachel Poertner
Susan Ashley
Low Mei Kheng
Jane Kizzia
Karen Pike,
   Karen Pike Photography, Hinesburg
RuthAnn Brown

73 Cal Baird
Joseph Verdyck
Rick Knobloch
Karen Ridges
Jennifer Rotenizer,
   Winston-Salem Journal
Laura Strassman

76 Gwen Young
Brian Clark
April Via
Briana LaFollette
Louise Shanley
Ann Wilbur

77 Donna Tweed
Ligia Besser
Danny Chou
Patrick Reddy,
   Cincinnati Enquirer
Elaine Massung
Andrea Potts

78 Sara Hayden
Caryl Bettez
Jason Cohn, www.jasoncohn.com
Ella Cummings
Carrie King
Erica Zwick

79 Tiba Daniela
Jason Cohn, www.jasoncohn.com
Nicole Pittard
Carrie Caldwell
Robin Barton
Colleen Finn

94 Bruce Strong, LightChasers
Renee Lapointe
Dan Hoke
Marisa Calhoun
Jamie Schwaberow,
   Rich Clarkson & Associates
Connie Patterson

100 Patty McNary
Peter Goldberg
Dennis Baker
Jenny Steele
Earl Richardson
Joyce Aldrich

104 Katariina Sutphin
Sterling Topping
Bill Ganzel
Jennifer Fearing
Sara Hayden
Marguerite Ruys

105 Laura Petri
Ingrid Rosenquist
Katie Avery
Bobby Model
Jill Greff
Anja Bles

108 Donna Meier
Gerrit G. Bradley
Mary Thoby
Kristen Pastir
Peter Casolino
Marga Partegis

109 Erika Westmoreland
Bruce Strong, LightChasers
Gigi Muracco
Costantino Molteni
Herrmann + Starke
Jennie Huettel

110 Shawn Perry
Jennifer Scott
Patrick Reddy,
   Cincinnati Enquirer
Caron Dube
Michael VanDerSanden
Chris Tapp

111 Terry Plouffe
Teresa Flores
Michele McDonald
Karen Spychalski
Keisha Sansevere
Andrea Rovere

112 Crystal Loh
Beth Reynolds,
  The Photo-Documentary Press, Inc.
Joyce Chin
Brigitte Davis
Beth Reynolds,
  The Photo-Documentary Press, Inc.
Sandra Wolven

113 Brenda DeWaele
Brenda DeWaele
Lynda Williams
Lucy Rosenthal
Beth Reynolds,
  The Photo-Documentary Press, Inc.
Lucy Rosenthal

114 Alex Brytak
Jeff Hatfield
Dave Hansen
Michele Conner
Carol Langford
Barbara Heinzmann

115 Bonnie Fricchione
Swing Yeung
James Shearer
Dave Hansen
Danielle White
Saranah Tandberg

116 Pete Savignano
Earline Brunt
Stephen Tuchow
Vicki Cronis
Robn Neufeld
Sherie Funke

117 Emily Ingram
Jason O'Neal
Tammy Rawlins
Tommy Grenander
Lynne Walsh
Ingrid Rosenquist

132 Sam Miller
Reann Lawler
Melanie Oliveros
Torsten Kjellstrand
Kerri Tokarz
Eric Martin

133 Shaune Grose
Lisa Yari
Bob Hammerstrom
Eric Yagoda
Karen Freed
Kristy Berg

134 Barbara Malatesta
Martha Cooper
Chris Fanning
Helen Pesho
A. Way
Karolina Einoriene

135 Sununta Uaprayoonvong
Kent Miller,
  The Bay City Times
Chris Balish
Sharon Wandler
Christine Keith
Paula Stevems

137 Lisa Olsen
Stephen Salpukas,
  Style Weekly
Heather Ajzenman
Kristine Adams
Sara Andrea Fajardo
Cathy Gregor

138 Jill Lipman
Lisa Riner
Justin Battle
Marina Malcevski
Edward Swoszowski
Nan Arthur

139 Eric Yagoda
Katie Lindquist
April Scott
Don Parsons
Wendy Shaw
Lucy Rosenthal

145 Kristy Berg
Brian Fogarty
Augusta Delisi
Sheila Heider
Alan Beymer
Patrick Fargo

150 Ann Beebe
Paul Rutherford
Danielle Adams
Emily Ingram
Rob Carr
Guy Fuchikami

151 Gladys E. Bywaters
Don Himsel,
  The Telegraph
Charmaine Thomas
Ellen Heise
Janet Worne,
  Lexington Herald-Leader
Jeff Moffett

170 Lisa Williams
Brian Wilcox
Kathryn Dinsmore
Jamie Gemmiti,
  Cross Road Studio
Sarah Peck
Chris Law

171 Josefine Stenudd
Linda DeLong
Nancie Battaglia
Michelle Hill
Rick Scull
Dan Cohen

172 Angela Wrenn
Ruth M. Wynne
Margo Baldrige
Renea Bosley
Nan McNurlen
Diane Lacey

173 Kristen Skibicki
Denise Belanger
Ed Franklin
Gloria Smith
Pamela Einarsen
Joan Harrison

174 Chad Musser
Stacey Cramp
Shannon Nolan
Jim Farkas
Steve Bly,
  Bly Photography
Deb Saunders

175 Zack Fisch
Maira Schriber
Gloria Saboff
Andrew A. Fuchs
C. Paige Burchel
Kerri Tokarz

176 Gary Little
Willie Harrell
Barbara Hames
Ronald W. Erdrich,
  Abilene Reporter-News
Linda Creel
Audrey King

177 Valerie R. Jones
Judith Berger
Daniel Richardson
Peter Gemei
Diana Kelley
Karen Rusch

178 Lan Luu
Jeanie Adams-Smith,
  Western Kentucky University
Courtney Caplette
Doreen Goldman
Erika Leigh Kruse
Nicole Turner

179 Laura Meyers
Jeanie Adams-Smith,
  Western Kentucky University
Joanna Obraske
Dawn Jastrem
Jill Gipson
Bonnie Fricchione

180 Kathy Porter
John Mastro
Lan Luu
Leah Hogsten
Heather Mckibben
Suzi Sacha

181 John Lehigh
Luke Gamache
Bianca Lebbink
Barbara Malatesta
Denny Carr, azimagery.com
Joy Streed

182 Angela Wrenn
W. Garth Dowling
Libby Dominguez
Diane Laws
Adrienne Koh
Noelle Boiteux

183 Sharon Coose
Barbara Leat
Lori Rosenberg
Mat Thorne,
  Western Kentucky University
Anca Schunk
Sara Hayden

Staff

Project Directors
Rick Smolan
David Elliot Cohen

Administrative
Katya Able, Operations Director
Chuck Gathard, Technology Director
Kim Shannon, Photographer Relations Director
Annie Polk, Publicity Manager
Alex Notides, Office Manager
John McAlester, Adminstrative Assistant

Design
Diane Dempsey Murray, Art Director
Bill Shore, Associate Art Director
Karen Mullarkey, Photography Director
Bill Marr, Senior Picture Editor
Sarah Leen, Senior Picture Editor

Editorial
Curt Sanburn, Senior Editor
Teresa L. Trego, Production Editor
Lea Aschkenas, Associate Editor
Korey Capozza, Associate Editor
Elise O'Keefe, Copy Chief
Will Hector, Copy Editor

Consultants
Mark Derr
Claudia Kawczynska and Cameron Woo,
    The Bark magazine
Dr. Sophia Yin, School of Veterinary Medicine,
    University of California, Davis

Interns
Erin O'Conner
William Cohen
Kara Cohen
Melissa Dulebohn

Morale Officers
Goose, the dog
Ezra, the dog
Pachinko, the puppy

Literary Agent
Carol Mann, The Carol Mann Agency

Legal Counsel
Barry Reder, Coblentz, Patch, Duffy & Bass, LLP

Accounting and Finance
Rita Dulebohn, Accountant
Robert Powers,
    Calegari, Morris & Co. Accountants
Eugene Blumberg, Blumberg & Associates
Arthur Langhaus,
    KLS Professional Advisors Group, Inc.

Web site and Digital Systems
Jeff Burchell, Applications Engineer
Luke Knowland, Designer

Senior Advisors
Jennifer Erwitt
Laureen Seeger
James Able
Maggie Cannon
Brad Zucroff
Megan Smith
Mike Moore
Brian Smiga
Lindsey Kurz
Tom Walker
Pres Williams
Phillip Moffitt
Michael Rylander
Tom Witt
Pete Hogg
Eric Schrier
Tom Ryder
Ted Rheingold
Ted Leonsis
Julie Wainright
Chris Fralic
Martha Danly
Liz Gebhardt
Betty Krause Taylor
Bob Angus
Barry Briggs
Carrie Wiley
Mat Gasquy
Jenny Kompolt
Leslie DuClos
Craig Gauger

Picture Editors
J. David Ake, Associated Press
Caren Alpert, formerly *Health* magazine
Simon Barnett, *Newsweek*
Caroline Couig, *San Jose Mercury News*
Mike Davis, formerly *National Geographic*
Michel duCille, *Washington Post*
Deborah Dragon, *Rolling Stone*
Victor Fisher, formerly Associated Press
Frank Folwell, *USA Today*
MaryAnne Golon, *Time*
Liz Grady, formerly *National Geographic*
Randall Greenwell, *San Francisco Chronicle*
C. Thomas Hardin,
    formerly *Louisville Courier-Journal*
Kathleen Hennessy, *San Francisco Chronicle*
Scot Jahn, *U.S. News & World Report*
Steve Jessmore, *Flint Journal*
John Kaplan, University of Florida
Kim Komenich, *San Francisco Chronicle*
Eliane Laffont, *Hachette Filipacchi Media*
Jean-Pierre Laffont, *Hachette Filipacchi Media*
Andrew Locke, MSNBC
Jose Lopez, *The New York Times*
Maria Mann, formerly AFP
Bill Marr, formerly *National Geographic*
Michele McNally, *Fortune*
James Merithew, *San Francisco Chronicle*
Eric Meskauskas, *New York Daily News*
Maddy Miller, *People* magazine

Michelle Molloy, *Newsweek*
Dolores Morrison, *New York Daily News*
Karen Mullarkey, formerly
    Newsweek, Rolling Stone, Sports Illustrated
Larry Nighswander, Ohio University
    School of Visual Communication
Jim Preston, *Baltimore Sun*
Sarah Rozen, formerly *Entertainment Weekly*
Mike Smith, *The New York Times*
Neal Ulevich, formerly Associated Press

Essay Writers
Mark Derr
Patricia B. McConnell
Michael J. Rosen

Chronicle Books
Nion McEvoy
Alicia Bergin
Shona Burns
Stephanie Hawkins
Jan Hughes
Tera Killip
Debbie Matsumoto
Deirdre Merrill
Steve Mockus
Doug Ogan
Jay Schaefer
Vivien Sung

Webshots
Narendra Rocherolle
Russ Novy
Diana Donovan
Nick Wilder
Anne Mitchell
Michael Jones
Milenko Milanovic
Andrew Yamashiro
Jeff Boissier
Julie Davidson
Sara Taunton
Penny Adams
Glenn Kimball
Renato Cedolin
Belynda Santos
Corey Herkender
Tara Geear
John Udasco
Teresa Derichsweiler
Martha Papalia

Edelman PR
Nicole Scott
Danielle Siemon

Acronym
Anton Konikoff, President
Tom Rielly, Vice President
Selina Allibhai,
    Search Engine Marketing Manager
Stephanie Hart, Project Manager